D1713499

PRAISE FOR
My Top 40 at 40: Making the First Half Count

Education

"This young adventurer shares seminal life experiences that resonate with the reader on many levels. I was reminded more than once of Tennyson's *Ulysses*—'To strive, to seek, to find, and not to yield.' Touching, funny, authentic, and inspiring, it's the ultimate 'no regrets' collection of vignettes and stories."

—Susan Nelson, Head of School at The Webb Schools of California

"What a fun romp into the world of a healthy, spirited, and ambitious man...Like *Chicken Soup for the Soul*, Loya's tales provide the perfect big brother sensibility for my children and take-life-by-the-horns nudge for myself."

—Kimberly Mitchell, Director of Partner Engagement, Teach For All – Argentina

"Loya has made the world his classroom, as both teacher and student. These great stories will inspire others to do the same."

—Seth Reynolds, Partner at The Parthenon Group

"Like an epic movie with adventure, drama, love, and wisdom—you won't want it to end. A completely new perspective on what is possible."

—Tony Byrd, Assistant Superintendent, Student Learning Division at Edmonds School District, WA

"A master storyteller turns 40 and shares his journey of fun, continual growth and global citizenship. There is an awesome smile on each page."

—Peter Briggs, Director of the Office for International Students and Scholars at Michigan State University

Travel

"Loya has seized every opportunity for adventure, and tells his stories with a healthy dose of self-deprecating humor. He inspires us to live life to the fullest."

—Jeff Shumlin, Co-Director of Putney Student Travel

Media and Entertainment

"Like those *Choose Your Own Adventure* books we read as kids, only Loya's adventures are real. A great page-turner."

—Arick Wierson, CEO of Occidental Atlantica and Record Emmy-Winning Former General Manager of NYC TV

Athletics

"Loya has packed a lot into his first 40 years—what a story he has to tell. I'm his admirer."

—Simon Clifford, Founder and CEO of Brazilian Soccer Schools and SOCATOTS

"When you've finished, you'll want to get to work on your own list of adventures!"

—Geoff Wheeler, Coach of Men's Soccer at Wesleyan University

Business, Technology, and Finance

"Loya runs his life like a kick-ass tech start-up: he's always on the hunt for new opportunities, exudes high-energy optimism, and makes every day count."

—Matt Compton, CEO of Shopigniter

"Forty stories of pure joie de vivre!"

—Richard Matusow, VP of Business Development at Sambazon

"A modern version of the Dr. Seuss book, *Oh, the Places You'll Go!*"

—John Addrizzo, Director at GlaxoSmithKline

MY TOP
40 *at* 40

Making the First Half Count

MY TOP 40 at 40

Making the First Half Count

A MODERN MAN'S STORY COLLECTION

XK PRODUCTIONS

Published by XK Productions, LLC. Elizabeth, NJ 07202. USA.

www.xkproductions.com

ISBN 978-0-9847637-0-2

Library of Congress Control Number: 2012935497
Subject Headings:
    1. Loya, Kari, date. 2. United States. Biography. 3. Travel. 4. Happiness.
    5. Self-realization. 6. Self-actualization (Psychology). 7. Quality of Life

Printed in the United States of America

First Edition

Book design by Shaila Abdullah

10 9 8 7 6 5 4 3 2 1

To Mom, Dad, Kristin, and Grandma Loya
for helping me dream and explore.

To Kamila—I can't wait to do the same for you.

To Ximena—Eres mi musa. Te amo y te adoro. Gracias por existir.

*Support education—10% of all author royalties will
be donated to educational not-for-profits.*

Obstacles are those frightful things you see when you take your eyes off your goal.

　—Henry Ford

There's a race of men that don't fit in,
　A race that can't stay still;
So they break the hearts of kith and kin,
　And they roam the world at will.
They range the field and they rove the flood,
　And they climb the mountain's crest;
Theirs is the curse of the gypsy blood,
　And they don't know how to rest.

　　—"The Men Who Don't Fit In," Robert W. Service

To scorn all strife, and to view all life
　With the curious eyes of a child;
From the plangent sea to the prairie,
　From the slum to the heart of the Wild.
From the red-rimmed star to the speck of sand,
　From the vast to the greatly small;
For I know that the whole for good is planned,
　And I want to see it all.

　　—"A Rolling Stone," Robert W. Service

CONTENTS

Part Four: Age 31-35

Part Five: Age 36-40

FOREWORD

My mentor at Oxford, International Baccalaureate Organization founder Alec Peterson, once told me that the test of a great education—or I might add, of a "modern man"—was that you could drop a person anywhere in the world and they would adapt just fine. Kari Loya would not only survive, he would thrive—and his collection of entertaining and inspiring stories make this abundantly clear.

Since Kari arrived at The Dwight School in 2003, I have had the pleasure of working every day with this practical visionary to help transform The Dwight School in New York City into a world-class institution with a global footprint. He has pushed me every bit of the way, combining the brain of an investment banker—rigorous analytical and strategic thinking—with the heart of a social worker whose genuine desire is to help others reach their potential.

When you read these stories, you'll discover someone who dares to dream, has the courage to take risks, challenges himself constantly in a variety of ways, and reflects deeply. Perhaps most important, however, he shows us that life can be a whole lot of fun if we want it to be. After all, the Chinese tell the story of two wise men who return to the world every 1000 years to evaluate humanity—in lieu of speaking, they simply laugh.

These pages will provide inspiration to all high school and college seniors to undertake their own fun, meaningful journeys during the next two decades. For the rest of us, regardless of age, the book is a reminder to seize the day, explore, and get our own experiences on paper to share with others. The clock is ticking—make it count.

Fondly,
Stephen H. Spahn
New York City

Stephen H. Spahn is Chancellor of The Dwight School in New York City and the Dwight Family of Schools, which operates campuses in London, Vancouver Island, Beijing, and Seoul. He serves on the Board of Directors of the International Baccalaureate Organization, based in Geneva. Since 1999, he has been a Partner in Quad Ventures, a private equity firm specializing in education companies. In 2011, Spahn received the prestigious Lewis Hine Distinguished Service Award for Service to Children and Youth.

Introduction:
Why My Top 40 at 40?

This book is my answer to the question, "How should I celebrate my fortieth birthday?" I wanted something fun and meaningful. I wanted something I could share with family and friends. And I wanted something that ultimately could smother the negativity of aging by offering an approach that says, "Bring it on!" What better way to celebrate a birthday than to collect favorite stories of your own adventures and share them with others? Six ideas underlie this belief:

Everyone loves a story. I once heard the Chilean novelist, Isabel Allende, recount her first year of teaching with a difficult class whose students had either severe learning disabilities or behavioral issues. With the sarcastic blessings of her colleagues still ringing in her ears, she entered the classroom and uttered these four magic words: "Once upon a time…" The room became silent—and she began her career not only as a great teacher, but as a gifted storyteller. The stories in this collection are the same ones I've told over campfires, late-night beers, and long road trips.

We write our own script. My favorite story of all-time is William Goldman's book *The Princess Bride* with its non-stop action and adventure from beginning to end. But why leave this for the imagination? Why not *live* it? We all have the chance to write *THE SCRIPT*—the script of our lives. As the old adage says, "Will you have enough stories to tell your grandchildren?"

Get it on paper. Bill Clinton once remarked that every American should write their memoirs. But "memoirs" can sound incredibly daunting, even a little boring, like an A-to-Z chronicle of every detail of our lives. But "stories" are *the best of*, the highlights, manageable nuggets which everyone can pen. Why wait until your nineties?

Do it…NOW! Randy Komisar's *The Monk and the Riddle* tells us that the traditional model of working hard for forty years in hopes of one day being able to do what we *really* want to do sets us up for disappointment. First, we might not even make it to old age, but second, when we finally do have that magical time—or money—we still might not know what we really want. You may have to do a lot of soul-searching and make some not-so-easy adjustments, but at least you will be headed in the right direction.

Age brings life lessons. When we turn forty—or any age—nothing is magically different. We've simply added another layer to our lives. Sandra Cisneros writes about this notion in her short story, "Eleven," where she compares aging to rings on a tree. Our outer layer may be different, but we are fundamentally the same person and can still have that giggle, that curiosity, that spark of the six-year-old. Wouldn't you, too, like to be the mighty redwood with fifteen hundred rings of experience and wisdom?

Enjoy life more year by year. I once heard the president of a prestigious college tell his graduates, "If you look back on these four years as the best four years of your life, we will have failed you." Brilliant. Every day is an opportunity to learn so that in each successive year—despite all that comes with growing older—we enjoy life even more. It's not about beauty, brawn, or assets. It's about cultivating character, fostering relationships, and developing the right mindset. I hope these stories show I'm on the right path.

Some may choose to read this book from cover to cover. Others may jump directly to stories with themes, places, or events of personal interest. Regardless, may something in this collection motivate you to run faster, think harder, explore further, reflect longer, dig deeper, or laugh louder. But most importantly, whether you're approaching forty, fifty, or any other milestone, I encourage you, too, to *bear-hug* your next birthday with your favorite stories.

PART ONE
Age 16-20

1

A Lesson in Humility
Getting hosed in my first job

When I graduated from high school, I beamed with pride— I was bound for an Ivy League college in the fall and eager to meet different people, explore new settings, and begin the next exciting chapter in life. Now all I needed was a summer job.

So on a weekday afternoon in June, I interviewed at Izzy's Pizza, my favorite pizza place in Eugene, Oregon. Even though I'd delivered newspapers from eighth grade through my junior year in high school, this was my first legitimate job interview. I arrived with polished penny loafers, ironed khakis, a pinstriped dress shirt, and a preppy Ralph Lauren tie. My resume on Ivory linen was still warm and crisp from Kinko's. And I'd rehearsed every possible question-and-answer scenario. The manager and I chatted and traded smiles for thirty minutes, then I politely thanked her and left, confident I had made a favorable impression.

As I walked out, another guy walked in—*the competition.* He wore ratty jeans, faded sneakers, and one of those black and white concert baseball sleeved t-shirts popular ten years back. He had long, stringy blond bangs that drooped over his eyes, which he cleared with a flick of his head as he came through the door. It seemed he hadn't even bothered to shower. *Wow!* I thought to myself, *What is that guy thinking?* My confidence now soared. Just as I expected, I was offered the job.

The following Monday I reported with Boy Scout punctuality for my first big day at work. And right next to me? Tim, the dude in the baseball sleeves, still wearing the same outfit from Friday. We both were assigned to the dish room.

The best part was that he was way, way better than I was. He was absolutely fearless. When the dishes came piling in, he'd corral them onto a tray the way a cowboy brings down a steer. Then he'd blast the water gun like his house was on fire, before shoving them into the dishwasher. Spray and steam shot everywhere. In the process, he'd drench himself from head to toe and grin at his battle scars as gobs of cheese and sauce dotted his pants, apron, and hair—you could have charged admission to see this human water park in action.

Next to Tim, I looked like a moron. I'd take a plate, scrub it slowly the way I'd always done at home, then carefully square it up on the rack before picking up the next one. I suffered dishwashing nightmares all summer. My technique improved over time, but I never came close to touching Tim. And I eventually faced the cold, wet truth: I'd been lucky to get the job.

Bonus Adventures: www.MyTop40at40.com

- *See graduation photo*
- *Hear Kari's commentary*

2

On the Trail of J. D. Salinger

A campus encounter

Perhaps the three most well-known and beloved Dartmouth College figures are Mr. Rogers, Captain Kangaroo, and Dr. Seuss—icons in the world of children's literature and entertainment. But when I was on campus in the early nineties, another celebrity drew more interest and piqued even more curiosity: J. D. Salinger of *Catcher in the Rye* fame. Although Salinger wasn't a graduate, he had chosen to settle down in an undisclosed location in the Upper Valley of New Hampshire when he left New York City in search of privacy. Rumor had it that he visited the campus frequently, though no one seemed to know what exactly he looked like. They simply knew he had created Holden Caulfield, one of the greatest adolescent literary heroes of all-time, prompting everyone to weigh in with their own

6

theory of his appearance and whereabouts—and, most of all, everyone secretly fancied meeting up with the giant.

One particular gentleman who appeared regularly on campus seemed to fit the bill. Like one of those painted, wood-carved, bearded sailor figures you see in coastal New England gift shops, this individual had a weathered face, wavy gray hair, gold-rimmed spectacles, and a khaki trench coat. He often walked his two labs around the Green, the field that marks both the center of Hanover and the hub of Dartmouth life. But no one knew his name. No one had heard him utter a word. Yet many of us suspected that this was our man. Especially me.

So one sunny spring morning of my sophomore year, as I ate breakfast with a buddy on a bench alongside the Green, I noticed our mysterious friend approaching slowly on the sidewalk behind us, dogs in tow, tracing his usual circuit. Hoping to start a conversation and resolve the mystery, I turned toward him, smiled, and when it seemed we had made eye contact said innocently, "Great day for a walk!"

This dignified gentleman, now just a couple meters away, paused as if deep in thought and took three measured steps toward me. He placed his hand on my shoulder, looked me squarely in the eye, and with the conviction of a man who has seen it all, declared, "Young man, *every* day is a great day for a walk…but *some* are finer than others!" His eyes twinkled and he walked on.

End Note: Less than a year later, the photo and obituary of this gentleman appeared in the local newspaper. He was not J. D. Salinger as many of us had thought, but another remarkable man in a remarkable college town. Oddly enough, nearly twenty years later, less than a day after I penned the first draft of this story on January 28, 2010, the reclusive author himself passed away at the age of ninety-one.

 Bonus Adventures: www.MyTop40at40.com
- *See Dartmouth Green*
- *Hear Kari's commentary*

3

An Olympic Summer
My dream internship

The morning after my twenty-first birthday party, I was hurting. It wasn't the booze—I'd only drunk two, maybe three, glasses of sangria the entire night. It was the sleep factor—I hadn't gotten any. After hours of dancing and some late-night churros, I had rolled into my apartment at seven in the morning *a la Española*, then showered and headed straight off to work *a la Americana*. Even though it was Saturday and I was exhausted, I couldn't complain. After all, I was in Barcelona. Working for Nike. At the Olympics. Life was pretty damn good.

My Spanish colleagues playfully dubbed me "El sobrino de Phil Knight"—the Nike founder's nephew, but as the low guy on the totem pole I did a little of everything. Need help translating a product catalog? *Kari!* An interpreter for the Spanish contractors building the twenty-third-floor penthouse Hospitality Suite? *Kari!* Someone to man Nike's Olympic promotional booth in El Corte Inglés, Spain's version of Macy's? *Dónde está Kari?* I even spent an afternoon passing out free Nike gear to tourists just below the illuminated fountains near Palacio Montjuic in a marketing arms race with archrival Reebok. I loved everything.

The internship had materialized the previous fall while I was living in Salamanca, Spain on Dartmouth's Foreign Study Program, my first travels outside the United States and British Columbia. One day after lectures on Lorca, Franco, and the Moorish influence on Spanish architecture, I took the three-hour train to Madrid to meet with Nike's general manager in Spain, a fellow Oregonian and the only American in their thirty-five employee, Barcelona-based operation. We hit it off—and I received then and there an offer to intern for ten weeks the following summer when the Games and the world rolled through town. I was psyched!

The anticipation of an Olympic summer helped soften the earlier sting of quitting soccer because of injuries—flat feet had given me back and hip problems. So while Dartmouth would capture two Ivy League titles in three years and finish in the top eight teams in the country, I had begun channeling thwarted athletic energy into the Spanish language. Everywhere I went I carried index cards listing hundreds of words and phrases and used every spare moment to study vocabulary, determined not to settle for "eat" when "scarf," "wolf down," or "nibble" might fit better. I forced my tongue through daily drills to shape my gringo mouth to the roller-coaster Romance language. I repeated entire Spanish newscasts, memorized Juan Luis Guerra lyrics, and recited dozens of Almodovar lines as if auditioning for his films. I even took my training camp south to Querétaro, Mexico, where I spent the winter as the teaching assistant on another Dartmouth program. By the time I arrived in Barcelona in June of 1992, I could defend myself well.

The fun increased when Nike executives began trickling in from around the globe. One was legendary marathoner, Alberto Salazar, who had briefly offered me advice four years earlier in Eugene. Shortly after breaking my ankle and determined not to lose soccer pre-season conditioning, I had begun walking every day on crutches, my foot bound in a cast, one mile to Spyglass Hill to do one-legged, hopping hill repeats up the steep, fifty-yard stretch near the top. Salazar appeared one day on the front steps of his home, which overlooked this section and advised me *not* to continue, suggesting it would lead to muscular imbalance and increase the likelihood of later injury. When a three-peat New York City marathon champion talks, you listen. I stopped the next day.

Then came the athletes. A week before the opening ceremonies, we shuttled out to the airport to pick up Australian marathoner Steve Moneghetti, Nike's first athlete to arrive and the last to compete. American sprinter Michael Johnson, the fastest two hundred and four hundred-meter runner in the world, began appearing regularly in the Hospitality Suite. Just hanging around these elite athletes who had devoted their lives and sculpted their bodies to one or two disciplines was inspiring. But it got even better. Before long, I was in the hot seat as the interpreter for many of the athletes during their press conferences, flipping between Spanish and English while reporters feverishly transcribed my words:

To Croatian basketball stars Tony Kukoc and Drazen Petrovic: "How will the difference in rules between the Olympics and the NBA affect play?"

To Cuban (and gold medal winning) high jumper Javier Sotomayor: "Mr. Sotomayor, who do you think is jumping the best right now?"

To Algerian Noureddine Morceli, favored to win the 1500 meters: "Will you try to set a world-record in tomorrow's final?"

Reading my words in the newspaper the next day made the experience all the more exhilarating.

But the biggest story of the 1992 Olympics was, of course, the arrival of the NBA Dream Team. Not the later versions of overpaid, under motivated players, but the original, THE Dream Team, who came with everything to prove: Michael, Magic, Larry, Sir Charles, Patrick, and the rest. While the NBA wives spent every day casually shopping (my colleague was charged with escorting them around the city), the players spent most of the two weeks as prisoners in their hotel behind automatic weapon-wielding guards to keep out both Basque terrorists from ETA and celebrity-gawking lunatics. On a rare sighting backstage after Nike's premier press conference with two thousand attendees that featured their two athletes rumored to fly—Michael Jordan and Ukrainian pole-vaulter Sergei Bubka, I stood a few feet from Jordan as he was interviewed by Ahmad Rashad. My boss and the cameraman were the only others there. As soon as the session ended, the world's greatest basketball player stood up with a long face and said flatly, "Yo, Cesar, let's get out of here." This was a chore, not fun. My boss tried to sneak Jordan out the back door to an escape mini-van, but inevitably he had to bulldoze through a circus of camera-toting throngs. I didn't envy Jordan one bit.

When not immersed in all-things-Nike and the Olympics, I explored the Greater Barcelona postcard: hopping on the back of a friend's motorcycle—every Spaniard owns a motorcycle or scooter at some point—and shooting up to Tibidao to run on the dusty trails overlooking the unfinished corncob spires of Sagrada Familia, the whimsical Parc Güell, and the other indelible marks of Antoni Gaudí; downing cuba libres, calamari, and *pa amb tomàquet*, the Catalunyan tomato bread, in the nearby beach towns of Sitges and Cadaqués; lounging for four days in August with a friend and her family in Menorca, an idyllic Mediterranean island, and boating in azure waters from grotto to grotto while the Iberian peninsula sleeps for the entire month.

But my biggest takeaway from the summer was how it all arose in the first place. An internship hadn't been advertised. I simply knew I loved the Olympics: the athleticism, the internationalism, and the drama—I had witnessed the barefooted South African Zola Budd and crowd-favorite Mary Decker Slaney collide in the 3000-meter final in 1984 in the Los Angeles Coliseum. I also knew I loved Spanish, so I brainstormed opportunities that might combine the two. And the clincher, my dad knew a former top Nike executive, an old friend, who reached out to the general manager in

Spain on my behalf and ultimately opened the door. I still remember the first line out of the smiling GM's mouth when we met at the hotel lobby in Madrid after my train ride from Salamanca: "Hi, Kari. So how do you know…?" It was an early lesson in social capital: What you know enables you to rise or fall, but *who you know* brings opportunity.

 Bonus Adventures: www.MyTop40at40.com
- *See Dartmouth soccer poster*
- *See Steve Moneghetti press conference*
- *Read Kari's brief Barcelona interview in* The Oregonian
- *Hear Kari's commentary*

PART TWO
Age 21-25

4

Teach For America
Learning as you go

When I joined Teach For America right out of college in 1993, I fancied myself the next Jaime Escalante (portrayed in the 1988 film *Stand and Deliver*), nose-to-nose with hardened gang members in the classroom and determined to employ tough love, creativity, an athlete's tenacity, and even charm to change their lives. But two days before I left for the summer training institute in Los Angeles, I got a call from the placement coordinator: "Would you be willing to teach primary?" *Primary?* I thought for a minute this might be TFA-code for an especially daunting assignment. Then it dawned on me: *You mean the little guys?* I couldn't remember Jaime Escalante sitting on the rug reading to his students, but my romantic Hollywood vision was secondary to my main purpose—to help.

"Sure," I answered, "Wherever you need me."

My motives for joining Teach For America, a relatively unknown program at the time that had been founded just three years earlier by Princeton graduate Wendy Kopp, were simple: to make a difference and to try teaching. I had enjoyed teaching Spanish language drill classes at Dartmouth under the tutelage of John Rassias, a legendary and innovative language professor who had even encouraged me to pursue a career teaching languages—something akin to Michael Jordan suggesting you go pro. But I had no interest in following the conventional route to certification, and Teach for America offered a unique, learn-as-you-go express entryway into the field.

That summer an army of five hundred equally passionate, driven, and perhaps naive corps members converged for six weeks on the beautiful, sprawling campus of UCLA, sandwiched between Westwood, Beverly Hills, and Bel Air—a stark contrast from the neighborhoods where we'd soon be assigned. Our apartments were spacious, our cafeteria was bountiful, and there was even a fifty-meter outdoor pool surrounded by sun-worshipping, European ESL summer school females. It was the good life. But we also immersed ourselves in Lee Canter assertive discipline workshops, whole language versus phonics discussions, and lesson-planning sessions late into the evening. It was incredibly inspiring to be with sharp, idealistic college graduates from across the country who wanted to become excellent teachers and were undaunted by the steep learning curve.

My own naiveté about more than teaching became evident the first weekend when a buddy and I, eager for a night on the town, ventured away from the safe confines of the UCLA campus to explore nightlife in LA. We found ourselves on a stretch of Hollywood Boulevard shortly after midnight where drunks and prostitutes hung out. But on the far corner of this seedy street shone the welcoming lights of a twenty-four-hour diner. We crossed the street and went in.

"Hi!" I greeted the fifty-year-old blond waitress, who had the haggard look of a third-tier Vegas hostess, hoping she could get our night back on track. "Can you tell us where there's a good bar around here?"

She studied us from head to toe, then asked in genuine disbelief, "Where're you boyzz from?"

Another long pause. The truth would have been too painful for our egos—I was from Eugene, Oregon and my buddy hailed from rural New Hampshire. We were no urban hipsters. So I simply replied, "Oh…we're, um, from UCLA."

This lady had been around the block a thousand times—and that particular block of Hollywood had it all. Like a skilled matador delivering the final *estocada*, she calmly and deftly ended our night out with "Boyzz…lemme call you a cab ride home."

That was it—no arguing. And when we stepped out the front door to wait for our taxi, she tugged us by the sleeves back inside, "No, wait *in here. Really.*" What would she have said if I told her that my friend and I—and five hundred others just like us—were preparing to head into the toughest inner-city and rural schools in America?

The following Monday I began student teaching in a split first and second grade class at the Cheremoya Elementary School on Franklin Avenue in Hollywood, not far from where we'd ended up three nights earlier. The school was part of the Los Angeles Unified School District and was made up entirely of Hispanic and Armenian children. Oddly, Cheremoya sat just below the fabled Hollywood sign and adjacent to the Mayfair Market, a frequent celebrity-spotting grocery store. Across the street rose the historic Chateau Elysee, which the Church of Scientology had purchased two decades earlier and recently converted into their flagship Celebrity Center.*

Each day I shadowed my forty-something mentor teacher, Kurt, trying to get my head around routines, transitions, and the actual first and second grade curriculum: letter names and sounds, shapes and colors, addition and subtraction, drawing and painting, singing and dancing along with a host of other things I hadn't thought about since, well, first grade.

While TFA corps members had been advised to dress professionally to command respect—we needed every advantage possible—Kurt sported cotton parachute pants, pink Converse high-tops, and a pastel t-shirt. He even boasted a golden caterpillar moustache. Also, he was openly gay. As I

---

* One Saturday, as part of a TFA get-to-know-your-school-neighborhood assignment that seemed more like a dare, two corps members and I visited the Institute, which some claimed turned kids into "zombies." Smiling attendants in powder blue suits led us into a twenty-seat theater lined with old books, the kind of room where someone with a silver beard and bow tie might be smoking a pipe. For fifteen minutes we watched a film on Thetans, engrams, and the rest of Ron Hubbard's philosophy while fighting off an unsettling feeling that Norman Bates, Rosemary, and members of their extended family were secretly watching us. We eagerly returned to liquor stores, pawnshops, and daylight.

came to learn, ninety-five of one hundred primary school teachers were generally female, and four of the five males were usually gay.

Despite his casual appearance, Kurt was amazing—he had the kids wrapped around his finger. He choreographed the movement of the children from the rug to their desks, from classroom to playground, and from activity to activity flawlessly. Every kid was always on task.

The final week of my student teaching it was my turn to lead the show. But it's one thing to step into the cockpit of a 747 mid-flight during a lull, and quite another to take off, navigate in turbulence, and land—you actually need to know how to fly. That same week I learned I'd soon be flying at Cleveland Elementary School in Pasadena, California with first and second graders.

At first glance, Cleveland Elementary School—where two-thirds of the students were African-American, one-third were Latino, and a few white Serbian refugees joined the mix—didn't fit my image of an inner-city school. I'd envisioned a soot-stained building surrounded by housing projects bathed in graffiti and wrapped in barbed wire and iron bars—the kind I'd seen in the distance in New York City or in the movies. Instead, palm trees lined both the school grounds and the yards of adjacent houses. The pine-covered San Gabriel Mountains provided a picturesque backdrop, soaring to over ten thousand feet. And the Rose Bowl—home of those majestic parades where floats were made entirely of rose petals!—sat just a half-mile to the west, flanking the wealthy enclave of San Marino.

But a half-mile on the other side of the stadium lay north-west Pasadena and Altadena, the local version of "South Central," where Bloods and Crips waged turf wars and crack houses abounded. When I volunteered to help with a start-of-the-year Food Drive, our principal, a no-nonsense African-American woman who had already effected great change at the school, pulled me aside: "Hun, you gotta change that shirt." My fire-engine red t-shirt shouted, "Gang." I changed the shirt.

When Day One finally arrived, I was ready—or at least as ready as I could be. Twenty-five six and seven-year-olds filed into my classroom, which I'd spent the prior week adorning with alphabet strips, number lines, months-of-the-year and days-of-the-week charts, and other visuals that might help conceal my lack of teaching experience. To these youngsters, I was Mr. Loya. And I was shaking more than they were.

While the students silently copied from the blackboard onto their paper "Today is the First Day of School!"—*set the proper tone and get the students on task immediately*, I'd been forewarned—I surveyed the scene: Jose struggled with just holding his pencil, carving at the paper as if he held a dagger; Nelly raced through the exercise skipping every other letter before proudly announcing, "I'm done!"; Jose Luis stared dreamily at the colorful pictures on the alphabet strip and required a gentle reminder to begin his work; and Saul, just outside the classroom, was tugging on his mom's leg and bawling, causing the other children to peer over their shoulders concerned he might know something they didn't.

For the next six hours, I applied every trick I'd gleaned from student teaching and the Summer Institute—and our day actually flowed smoothly. Even Saul eventually joined us. We read *Brown Bear, Brown Bear* on the rug and the kids drew their favorite animal. We reviewed and acted out the classroom rules. We assigned classroom jobs, like turning off the lights, sharpening the pencils, and watering our lone plant. We toured the school, including the cafeteria, the nurse's office, and everyone's favorite—the playground. We sang, stomped, and clapped using my entire repertoire of children's songs, and on two occasions to fill an unanticipated fifteen-minute void, I resorted to "Simon Says."

When the bell finally rang at two thirty that afternoon, I'd done it—I'd triumphed! I'd survived the much-dreaded first day of teaching. Two colleagues came by to congratulate me. *That wasn't so bad!* I thought, patting myself on the back in brief celebration. But then the brutal realization hit me along with the worst panic of my life: I'd just spent six weeks preparing for one day of school, and *oh... my... God*—I had to go back for a SECOND day tomorrow. *Six more hours of lessons to plan? When would I ever sleep? And how many games of Simon Says could I play?*

That first day kicked off one of the most challenging and thrilling years of my life, where every night I scrambled to create content and organize lesson plans (pre-internet); where every hour in the classroom my management skills were put to the test like a CEO under fire; and where every moment I bore the awesome responsibility of inspiring and leading thirty little minds forward, some more eager and able to advance than others.

Perfectionism? *Small Victories!* became my mantra: work toward that "A" with our morning journal and calendar routine; hope for an occasional standout lesson in science or math, art or language; but accept the humbling fact that several lessons every day would probably bomb. If it was too hard, the kids would fidget; If it was too easy, they'd finish in ten minutes, leaving a dangerous window for pinching, spitting, and other forms of six-year-old trouble. Countless other challenges arose: *Why did only half the class have their tanagrams for our math lesson? And what was that sticky substance on the floor that now attracted more attention than my talk about plant parts?* It was mind-boggling how many ways one little lesson could get derailed.

The toughest part was accepting that it was generally my fault—I simply hadn't prepared enough. Yet I'd *never* have enough hours in the day. What I needed, I decided, was a longer term perspective: take care of myself (sleep, eat well, exercise, socialize), plug away, and take pride in small improvements lesson by lesson, day by day, and week by week. As a consolation, while a first grader's attention span was about ten minutes, mine was only eight, giving me a two-minute head start throughout the day.

Every week I connected with mentor teachers whose experience and mastery of their craft was truly inspiring: Mrs. Kincey, the veteran from Altadena in the first grade classroom next door, whose magical aura lifted the spirits of every child she taught; Ms. Shoemaker, the bilingual doctoral student from UCLA in the second and third grade classroom across the Quad, who worked harder than anyone to find creative, practical solutions to instructional challenges; and Mr. Shepherd, a rare heterosexual jock whose life-long passion was to teach first grade and who could convince you that geoboards, cloud formations, and the hard and soft "C" sounds were the most fascinating things in the universe. Even T-Money, the school janitor and my cultural attaché, was a help. He affectionately nicknamed me T-Baby and kept me *real* by dropping off cassette tapes with the latest Snoop Dogg raps.

Every week I also reconnected with my roommates and TFA colleagues at other schools who were climbing the same mountain: sixth grade teachers dealing with teen pregnancies; tenth grade English teachers tackling illiteracy; primary grade teachers battling classroom management. Their intelligence, commitment, fire, and most importantly, ability to laugh at themselves were equally inspiring.

In my third year, thirty-four first and second graders—yes, thirty-four—packed into my classroom. I hit my stride mid-year. I saw clearly where we were headed with the curriculum and loved mapping out units and detailed lessons on the rainforest, pumpkins, and other grade-relevant themes; I knew each of the kids well—their strengths and weaknesses—and anticipated potential pitfalls of any lesson, and when things didn't work out the way I wanted, I kept my cool and my humor. Bored with this week's vocabulary words? Time for a quick group stretch before inviting three students to write the words on the board while everyone else wrote them in the air. An unplanned block of twenty minutes? A chance for free-exploration with math manipulatives, student-produced stories, or another of the dozen learning centers we'd created. Missing materials? An opportunity for group problem-solving and role-playing—"Oh, no! I apologize. I didn't bring enough toothpicks for everyone. Raise your hand if you can suggest how we might resolve this?" And sticky mystery substances? Merely fuel for another wonderful discussion—"What do you think it is? Why? How did it get there? How could we prevent this from happening again?" By June, every one of my kids, most of whom had started the school year with minimal letter recognition, could read—my proudest accomplishment from those three years.

My own journey came to an emotional end when I organized an end-of-year graduation potluck for my students and their families in Brookside Park, just south of the Rose Bowl. During dinner I presented an award to each student for something that made him or her stand out. As I handed out the last prize, a stream of black, silver, gold, and brass bodies suddenly flowed all around me like giant, bejeweled ants invading the party. Only these ants carried violins, guitars, and trumpets…Mariachis! This group of families from the lowest socio-economic rungs of society had pooled their limited resources to hire a Mariachi band in my honor to say thank you. That's as good as it gets.

BONUS ADVENTURES: www.MyTop40at40.com

- *See Kari's classroom at Cleveland Elementary*
- *Watch LA Fox News World Cup Assembly video clip*
- *See mariachis at graduation potluck*
- *Hear Kari's commentary*

5

The Frozen Rattlesnake
Weirdness everywhere

I've dodged four-foot rattlesnakes while biking and running in the hills of Los Angeles. I've savored rattlesnake sausage paired with a fine Chardonnay at the Explorers' Club in New York City. But my favorite rattlesnake story is about the frozen rattler I randomly encountered at a birthday party.

During my first year living in Los Angeles, right out of college, I was invited to what sounded like a cool weekend party up in the dusty foothills of the San Gabriel Mountains behind Pasadena. A friend worked at the Armory in Old Town Pasadena and mentioned that her Armenian artist friend was celebrating his birthday with a pig roast on his ranch. *Artist? Pig roast? Ranch?* That guaranteed an entertaining evening.

You can arrive fashionably late to a party, Latin American late, or just late. We were just plain late. The open-air dance floor still held a hundred guests dancing and mingling, but the pig—splayed out in the middle of a banquet table on the edge of the dance floor—had already been devoured by lions, hyenas, vultures, and now had passed on to the flies. In the middle of the crowd stood a stout gentleman with a Santa beard, an elaborate robe, and an oversized Carmen Miranda fruit hat. This was evidently the Birthday Boy.

My roommate and I approached our host and when the gentleman turned to face us, my buddy, a consummate black-tie diplomat, thanked the man for hosting the wonderful party and wished him a happy birthday. An uncomfortably long pause followed. The robed artist squinted his eyes, turned his icy glare toward me, then addressed us both with a scowl, "*Who* are you—and *what* are you doing here?" as if we had scaled a security fence to crash his party.

As we stammered a reply about being friends of so-and-so, he simply turned his back and resumed his conversation. Had it been an apartment in New York City, the awkwardness of such a greeting would have compelled us to leave. But this was a sprawling, dimly lit compound cluttered with railroad ties, scrap metal, bales of hay, and tons of other random objects that made the place feel part junkyard, part gallery, part dude ranch. The hundred-plus colorful guests filled in the gaps. So we naturally did what any other party crasher would have done—we disappeared among the crowd and mingled. And we explored.

We wandered the dirt paths from tent to tent and cabin to cabin. After a few minutes, we came across an open door revealing dozens of paintings—all nudes—hanging on the walls and stacked on the floor. Just outside, we struck up a conversation with a young man in his twenties, a magician who lived on the compound and performed regularly at the Magic Castle, the well-known, eccentric, members-only club located in a Victorian mansion in Hollywood. He introduced us to his beautiful girlfriend, a model, who lived with him in the adjacent cabin. She and other models living on the compound often posed nude for Birthday Boy. In fact, we recognized her *face* from some of the paintings we'd just seen.

He invited us inside his cabin where the first thing we saw was his three-foot pet iguana perched on a bunk bed, flicking its tongue to greet us. *A magician. A nude model. A pet iguana.* This was quickly turning into a strange Brothers Grimm adventure—and then it got even better.

Our magician friend told us that a lot of rattlesnakes lived in those hills. In fact, just that morning he'd encountered a big one at the outhouse when he'd gone to take a leak.

"So what did you do?" we asked.

"Well, I was just going to kill it," he began, "but I *really* wanted a new pair of boots…"

As his voice trailed off, he turned toward a refrigerator in the middle of his cabin and opened the freezer bin at the bottom. He hoisted up a pillowcase, then pulled it back slowly to reveal a coiled, perfectly-preserved, three-foot frozen rattlesnake. He grabbed the snake just below the head and handed it to me, and I, in turn, grabbed it by its neck and did what I guess you're supposed to do when you grab a frozen rat-tlesnake—I shook it. *Trrrrrrrrrrrrrr! Trrrrrrrrrrrrrrr!* It was the ultimate, cryogenically-engineered maraca. This guy had ensnared the venomous creature in a pillowcase, then froze it to death to avoid any blemishes on its skin. He beamed with pride knowing he'd earned himself some fantastic new boots. I never say never, but I'll be astonished if I ever see another frozen rattlesnake in my lifetime.

As a postscript, three years later I read the Nobel Prize-winning scientist Richard Feynman's wonderful autobiog-raphy, Surely You're Joking, *Mr. Feynman.* One of the last chapters, "But is it Art?" began as follows: "Once I was at a party playing bongos, and I got going pretty well. One of the guys was particularly inspired by the drumming. He went into the bathroom, took off his shirt, smeared shaving cream in funny designs all over his chest, and came out dancing wildly, with cherries hanging from his ears. Naturally, this crazy nut and I became good friends right away. His name is Jirayr Zorthian; he's an artist." I chuckled in disbelief upon realizing that Birthday Boy had been none other than Feyn-man's buddy, Zorthian. Small world.

 Bonus Adventures: www.MyTop40at40.com

- *Visit www.zorthianranch.com*
- *Visit www.magiccastle.com*
- *See (unfrozen) rattlesnake photo in San Gabriel Mountains*
- *Read* Surely You're Joking, Mr. Feynman *(Richard Feynman)*

6

The Mud Volcanoes
On the edge with the most interesting man I know

To jump on a moving freight train, you must first match its speed. This could exceed fifteen miles per hour, requiring an all-out Olympic sprint while navigating obstacles such as railroad ties, rocks, and an awkward slope. As the do-not-try-this-at-home warning bells reach a crescendo inside your head, you reach for something on the train to grab onto—a vertical bar, a horizontal handle, anything. Finally, with equal proportions of strength and faith, you hoist yourself like a Cirque du Soleil gymnast onto the charging steel dragon.

Of our adventurous foursome—an anthropologist, an amusement park designer, a Hollywood producer, and me—I was the only one to pass all three tests. *Chug! Chug! Chug!* For ten exhilarating seconds, I roared forward through one-hundred-sixty-foot-tall, space-age wind turbines just west of Palm Springs in the San Gorgonio Pass Wind Farm, feeling like a test pilot on the perfect backdrop for a George Lucas film. But this particular rush wouldn't last long. *Volcanoes. Mud Volcanoes.* That was our real purpose. And that meant…dismounting.

I blocked out imagery of Hollywood heroes, villains, and expendable extras careening down embankments after hurling themselves from a train. With the ground blurring below, I spotted a clearing fifty yards ahead and timed my landing. Bam! I pounded the ground in my best Road Runner impression and successfully decelerated, my feet now afire. High-fives awaited me from everyone in our crew, including our grinning ringleader, Wallace, the most fascinating person I'd ever known.

Wallace and I had met a year earlier, in 1994, at a Brazilian samba dance class in Santa Monica during my first year living in Los Angeles, but we really got to know each other on a six-hour drive to San Francisco where our troupe would perform in the Memorial Day Carnival parade. I learned that Wallace had grown up in poverty in Southern California, with his father in and out of prison, and his mother moving him to a lesbian commune for greater stability. At sixteen, he joined a group of evangelical Christian performers that visited retirement centers, where he asked all the old folks one simple question: "How do you lead a good life?" Over and over, he heard the same theme: Few regretted anything they had done, yet everyone regretted things they had not done.

Wallace took that insight to heart and enrolled in college, majored in anthropology, and graduated valedictorian taking only Tuesday and Thursday classes *because his free time was too important.* His major interest was ethnobotany—how humans use plants—and his specialty was psychotropes, namely hallucinogenic plants. When he pursued his masters back East, he selected a thesis topic related to surfing so he could do his winter research in sunny Southern California. His already non-traditional resume was padded in between with everything from driving taxis in Venice Beach to copywriting for the porn industry in the San Fernando Valley, gathering material that would have made Jack London and Jack Kerouac envious. He threw himself 150 percent into everything and treated every uncanny experience—often with himself as human guinea pig—as an opportunity to learn, and for each experience, he'd devour every related book and scientific journal, often in multiple languages.

His remarkable story sprang to life as we crossed the Grapevine and descended into the San Joaquin Valley, thirty miles south of Bakersfield. I'd always blown through this bleak stretch as quickly as possible with the tunes cranked.

"Desolate, huh?" I casually remarked, unaware I'd just triggered one of a thousand lectures swimming around in Wallace's head.

"I love this place!" he responded, like a kid at the gates of Disneyland.

Over the next thirty miles, we stopped a half-dozen times to collect plant samples. *Plant samples…for fun!* What started innocently enough—wild mustard leaves for salad, aloe vera for a cut on my leg—quickly advanced to semi-toxic, not-for-kids material worthy of Carlos Castaneda, such as *Datura* for tea as brewed by the Chumash and other local tribes for vision quests, and *Artemisia absinthium*, reputedly an aphrodisiac which caused your skin to tingle when smoked.

The next morning, with my head still spinning from Wallace's tales, we met our samba troupe in San Francisco's Mission District, dressed as if we'd be shot from a cannon, with tight red jumpsuits, green and yellow feathers flying from our heads, and floral capes floating behind. When the Brazilian percussion kicked into gear and our troupe began weaving and wiggling through the streets, self-doubt crept into my head: *Dude, what are you doing?* But just then a woman a few feet away, behind the ropes on the curb, now packed three people deep, clenched her fists in the air and screamed, "Shake it, babyyyyyyy! SHAAAAAAke it!" This was just the encouragement I needed to cut loose and go for it. I became a human earthquake, matching Wallace in his own lack of inhibition one row away, shaking my hips, shoulders, and every other wobbly body part to the delight of the crowd.

Six months later, I'd progressed from samba dancing in San Francisco to hopping a freight train in the Southern California desert. I was now ready for the mud volcanoes.

Wallace had stumbled upon a reference to "those fabulous mud volcanoes" while perusing a California travel guide from the early 1900s—precisely the random sort of thing Wallace would read. Subsequent guidebooks, however, made no mention of the sight. Piecing clues together about the latitude and longitude and literally knocking on one farmhouse door after another, Wallace had eventually tracked down these geological oddities near the eastern edge of the Salton Sea, three hours east of Los Angeles. With the off-kilter zeal of Willy Wonka, he was now guiding us to this hidden treasure trove.

Driving along the back roads abutting the Salton Sea was like cruising through the town of Nowhere. The water, sky, and barren tracts of land were various hues of gray that melded into oblivion. Aside from an occasional tumbleweed somersaulting across our path, no life existed. Nothing. Just the hissing of the wind. We crept forward as Wallace tried to get his bearings. Then, we heard something: *Ga-bloop. Blop. Ba-bloop.* Our conversation halted. *Ga-bloop. Ga-blop. Bloop. Bloop.* There it was again! These were the same noises you might hear if you downed a pot of Louisiana chili, guzzled a Starbuck's *grande* Bold, then pounded a couple draft beers—noises that warned everyone to back off. Twenty yards from the road, in the middle of a dirt patch, were several *salses*—the geological term for mud cones—protruding a few feet above the ground. Nearby, pools of latte-brown water bubbled and gurgled. Steam rose from both mounds and pools, and every few seconds a volcano coughed gobs of mud up into the air. We got out of the car and stared, mouths agape.

But what exactly do you do with a mud volcano? Answering with an exclamation point, Wallace peeled off his clothes and in less than a minute had oozed his naked body into the mouth of one of the cones so that only his head appeared. *Jesus Christ! What the hell do we do if*

36

it sucks him down? I thought, suddenly imagining Wallace as the unfortunate protagonist of a gooey Jules Verne journey to the center of the earth. "Cult Feeds Victim to Mother Earth in Bizarre Desert Sex Ritual," the tabloids would read. But after two minutes of watching him frolic in the warm, thick mud without vanishing, the rest of us lightened up, stripped, and joined him. We adopted neighboring cones, christening this newfound Mud Volcanoes Spa and Resort.

Squeezing into the narrow shaft of a mud volcano feels strangely pure, pornographic, and, at least initially, like the losing end of a serious bet. The opening barely swallowed my body. Warm, sulfur-scented, viscous mud fought back as I pushed my toes, feet, and finally legs downward. My testicles, meanwhile, couldn't decide whether to relax or retract in this strange new medium. The sides were stiff, but malleable, like a Silly-Putty sleeping bag. I burrowed my way deeper up to my chest. As my confidence grew, I sank so that just my head emerged from this odd womb, as close as I'll ever get to reliving my birth. I closed my eyes and savored nature's full-body steam and mud massage.

Climbing out of the cone was equally celestial. Our bodies were now caked with one-half inch of earthy armor, making us look like odd superheroes. We plunged into the pools to remove mud from every orifice, then packed back into the car exactly six hours after beginning our journey that morning in Los Angeles.

As my mind drifted to a hot shower, a cold beer, and a well-deserved afternoon nap, Wallace was already at the wheel promoting our next stop, like an infomercial teasing you with a "But wait—there's more!"

"Guys," he announced, "We're just twenty miles from Salvation Mountain, Leonard Knight's crazy art project!" Of course we hadn't heard of this, but then again, we'd never heard of the mud volcanoes either.

"You're gonna love it!" Wallace assured us with a hearty laugh. We all smiled gamely, then our car shot further east into the desert.

 Bonus Adventures: www.MyTop40at40.com

- *See Kari and Wallace with samba troupe*
- *See mud volcanoes*
- *Hear Kari's commentary*

7

A Guatemalan Adventure
You never know what's next

Part I: Volcanoes

The first night of a trip often sets the tone for the rest of a journey. So in July of 1994, when I spent my first night in Guatemala squeezing out some shut-eye in the back seat of a cab, it was like begging for a week of pirates, prisons, and prostitutes.

I hadn't planned it that way, of course. My primary destination was Costa Rica, but frequent flyer miles allowed me one free stopover, and for a twenty-two-year-old, "free" is synonymous with "nirvana"—Free pizza. Free beer. Free stopover in Guatemala. Yet now because of delays, I landed in Guatemala City well after midnight, complicating my original plan to hire a cab directly to Antigua, two hours away in the mountains. The lone cabbie with whom I spoke agreed to drive me, but—there's always a *but* in Latin America—first he needed to deliver something to a friend who would be arriving at the airport at six the next morning. Besides, he assured me, the drive would be much safer and prettier in the morning. Why didn't I just sleep in his taxi and we'd leave first thing the next day? It's not like I had a lot of options, so I agreed.

After the worst night of sleep of my life in which my sleeping quarters became a side-show for every late night airport employee, I was relieved to finally make it to Antigua the next morning. Surrounded by verdant mountains and overlooking the tranquil waters of Lake Atitlán, this indigenous town lured many backpackers who often relocated there indefinitely. For the short-termers like me, Antigua boasted the proverbial street of tourist agencies with their sidewalk easels displaying the latest, greatest excursion photos. One in particular caught my eye—a hike to the rim of Volcán Pacaya, an active volcano spewing molten lava.

One of the best things about travelling outside the US is that you can try things—like hiking to the rim of an active volcano—that would never fly back home. Of course, all those pesky rules and regulations in the States that often seem to spoil the party also serve to keep our limbs intact and ensure that we'll be back at the party tomorrow instead of an unfortunate statistic. But for those willing to venture beyond our borders and flirt with danger...

That night on the rooftop of my five-dollar hostel I struck up a conversation with a Romanian traveler and mentioned I'd signed up to climb Pacaya. *Pacaya?* It was as if I'd put a hex on him. Just the night before, he had shared a room with an Italian tourist who had returned from the Pacaya outing traumatized. Apparently when the group began the final ascent toward the rim of the crater, the winds unexpectedly shifted and molten rocks showered down. The guides were the first to run. Everyone else followed in a panic. While the Italian scrambled down the slope, one of the rocks hit his backpack and melted right through it, warping his heavy-duty camera. At this point, another hostel resident fanned the flames further, "Yeah, and last week on Pacaya a group was attacked by some rebels, and an American woman was raped." He told us that an armed guard now escorted each entourage.

Now I was even more intrigued. Early the next morning I joined the Pacaya excursion which began with one of those three-hour "prepare-to-meet-your-maker" bus rides on winding dirt roads into the mountains that every backpacker has experienced at least once. When we finally reached the trailhead, we were thankful to be alive. Now the *real* excursion would begin. A dozen of us set off on the trail with our youthful guide in the lead and our armed guard in the rear, a wizened septuagenarian with a rickety rifle who inspired as much confidence as our bus driver.

After two hours of hiking through lush vegetation, we reached a clearing just above tree line. Dusk had already fallen, yet we could still make out the conic silhouette of Pacaya, rumbling intermittently across the way. When clouds suddenly enveloped us, I figured our hike would end here. Instead, our guide shouted, "*Vámonos!*" and we started across the pumice field *directly toward the cone, directly toward the rumbling*. Visibility was terrible. I could barely see my own feet, let alone the person in front of me. We were now hiking directly up the cone. Every thirty seconds or so, the volcano rumbled, the ground trembled, and steam shot out from fissures on the ground.

We proceeded like this in silence for thirty minutes, like a scene out of some terrible account of a Mayan human sacrifice. Every few steps we'd hear the rumble, and every few minutes the clouds would thin out, revealing the lights of Guatemala City off in the distance. Then the trail leveled off—we had reached the summit, which turned out to be a hundred yards away from another summit, the one with the crater in the middle. We spread out on the ground like Fourth of July picnickers and spent the next half hour admiring nature's fireworks—lava and incandescent rocks shooting up from the crater. The steam puffs from nearby crevices kept us warm, and the city lights gleamed on the horizon. I'd rebounded well from that first night in the cab. What next?

Part II: Pyramids

The thrill continued when I flew off to northeastern Guatemala to visit Tikal National Park, the capital of Mayan civilization and the largest indigenous ruins in the Americas. Imagine one pyramid-temple after another smack in the middle of the jungle, a place to inspire the next generation of Indiana Joneses. Keel-billed toucans, parrots, and spider monkeys flew overhead; anteaters and coatis foraged among the plants; tarantulas and scorpions crawled along the ground; fer-de-lances—nicknamed *dos pasos* after the number of steps you'd take once bitten before dying—slithered somewhere in the understory. And if you were lucky, you might even glimpse an ocelot, puma, or jaguar.

One small entry in my *Let's Go* guidebook had piqued my interest before the trip. It mentioned that if you approached the park guides in the *right* way just as the park was closing, you might be allowed to spend the night inside—even on one of the spectacular temples. That was enough to fire my curiosity.

So at the end of a hot and humid day of exploring, as the sun set and the visitors shuffled toward the exit, I wandered along a path in the opposite direction and lay low for fifteen minutes. I thought I was in the clear, but just then two pistol-toting guards turned the corner.

"Isn't it possible to spend the night *inside the park*?" I inquired innocently in Spanish.

"No, no, not at all," they replied in unison and began to escort me back toward the exit.

"Okay," I thought to myself, "Well, at least I tried." I can't say I was disappointed—the idea of spending the night alone in the jungle had sounded a hell of a lot better at a barbecue in Los Angeles than when I was actually standing there with night falling.

But then something strange happened. As we trudged along, one of the guards motioned off to the side and said, "That's a pretty decent place to camp…" I wasn't sure I had heard him correctly.

"…and some folks like to camp over there," he continued, confusing me further. They stopped abruptly to face me while pointing to yet another location. It was clear that this was the moment. I wished I had taken *Bribery, Blackmail, and Extortion 101* as a college elective—I had never bribed anyone in my life and now I suddenly felt like a middle-schooler on a first date. *What was my next move?* I thanked them politely for their suggestions, leafed through my wallet, and offered them the few bills I had—roughly ten US dollars of Guatemalan *quetzales*. Their eyes showed disappointment, so my awkward dance continued.

"Well, um…uh…let me…uh…see if I have anything else…in here…" I said as I fumbled through the side pocket of my backpack.

I retrieved a handful of silver *centavos*, crumpled bus ticket stubs, a few odd receipts, and a bottle of Johnson & Johnson sunscreen that had leaked onto everything. Now the dance was not only awkward, but messy. When I extended my gooey hand toward them with this additional bounty, they shrugged their shoulders, and settled for the first offering. Then they disappeared. *I did it!* But just as I was swelling with pride, I began to feel like the dog that had finally caught the car—*Jesus! What now?* My jaw was now locked firmly on the bumper.

Few things are more exhilarating than walking through Tikal at night alone. Every rustle, every crunch, every shadow rocketed my pulse. The massive roots of the *ceiba* (kapok) trees—just hours earlier an endless source of amazement— now crisscrossed every path like vipers in an Edgar Allen Poe story. If someone had come out of the jungle or shouted "boo!" I would have jumped to California.

I bee-lined for Temple IV, the highest perch in the park soaring two hundred thirty feet above the plaza floor. To climb up the temple required leaving the main path, which meant disregarding the mantra of every horror movie audience: *Don't leave the main trail!* I navigated a short, steep path through the understory and up a series of *Raiders of the Lost Ark* ladders through the canopy with the dim light of my headlamp doing more harm than good, transforming branches and vines into beasts and confusing my senses with leaping shadows. Beyond the small circle of light where I could see, I knew there was a hell of lot more that I couldn't.

After what felt like ages, I finally reached the upper ledge of the temple overlooking the entire jungle. I turned the corner toward the front and was amazed—and relieved!—to discover two other backpackers, a couple of Dutch guys. My spirits lifted—I was merely late for the party! And what a party, with the symphony of toucans, howler monkeys, tree frogs, and other exotic creatures performing in surround sound. To top it off, heat lightning danced across the night sky. With the thirteen-hundred-year-old carved stone as my bed and my *Let's Go* guidebook as my pillow, I lay down to sleep a couple of hours later. Was it a good night's sleep? Absolutely not. Was it a spectacular night's sleep? You bet.

Part III: Fiery Planes

As I sat on the plane in Flores the next afternoon waiting to take-off, I daydreamed about my action-packed week in Guatemala. *Antigua. Pacaya. Tikal.* I felt like I'd been gone a month. Now I was looking forward to a quick flight to the capital, a quiet night of real rest, and then an early morning flight to Costa Rica. I started to doze off…

An hour later I was startled awake by an announcement—we still had not taken off—that we should all de-board the plane. Mechanical difficulties. A few folks grumbled, but most of us took it in stride and filed out onto the tarmac. Since this was the last flight of the day, the terminal itself had already closed and we couldn't get back into the airport. So we all just sprawled out on the concrete in the balmy twilight snacking, chatting, or napping.

I struck up a conversation with a surfer from Santa Cruz who had a Frisbee, and we spent the next hour swapping stories and tossing the disc back and forth, completely carefree, thirty yards from the airport terminal and thirty yards from our plane. I'd even forgotten about our delay. Then, I heard what sounded like a giant blowtorch and spun around to see the plane's engine shooting out flames, and three mechanics in jumpsuits—the Guatemalan Larry, Curly, and Moe—sprinting away from the fireball.

"Well," commented one passenger matter-of-factly, "I guess we're not flying back tonight."

The buzz and panic began about how we would make our connecting flights. If we had to spend the night in Flores and catch a morning flight to Guatemala City, many of us would miss our international flights.

Just when the babble reached a crescendo, we heard the friendly voice of our stewardess, this time blaring through a handheld megaphone: "Ladies and gentlemen, everything has been repaired. You may now board the plane."

What? We'd all seen the fireball. We'd all seen the mechanics run for their lives. To reboard that aircraft would be like seeing Jaws attack, then going for a swim. It seemed like Russian roulette. Yet we all got in, going with the flow.

When we finally landed, everyone thanked the powers that be for arriving safely, but our prospects for finding a room in Guatemala City on a Saturday night were bleak. Santa Cruz surfer and I teamed up to look for lodging. Hostel Number one? *Completo.* Hostel Number Two? *Lo siento.* Hostel Number Three? *Lo siento mucho.* After tramping around with our backpacks for another hour, we finally found a hostel manager who took pity on us. He couldn't give us a room, but for half-price he could make another...*arrangement.*

I couldn't have framed the trip any better. If my first night had landed me in the back of a cab, my last night scored me one-half (we shared!) of a dingy, crusted-over, foam mattress under the stairwell of a youth hostel, only three feet from the one common malodorous bathroom that everyone in the city seemed to visit that night. But hey—at least no pirates, prisons, or prostitutes.

 Bonus Adventures: www.MyTop40at40.com
- *See the view from the bed*
- *See the Jungle Party to celebrate the trip*
- *Hear Kari's commentary*

8

The Voice of God
Meeting the King of Voice-overs

When it comes to housing, I peaked too early. Right out of college, three buddies and I scored a fantastic pad in Los Feliz in the eastern part of the Hollywood Hills. Our two-story house had spectacular views: the Griffith Park Observatory, the beautiful Pacific Ocean, and even Catalina Island in the distance. Two large balconies overlooked our backyard where deer, skunks, jackrabbits, and coyote routinely scampered, belying our proximity to downtown. We even enjoyed a fireplace upstairs—surprisingly useful during an LA winter—and another downstairs in the master bedroom, better known as the Bruce Wayne bachelor's lair. And the real irony? As starting elementary school teachers, we each earned twenty-six thousand dollars, yet comfortably afforded our five hundred dollar share of the rent. It was a bargain.

Then there were the neighbors—Flea of the Red Hot Chili Peppers lived just down the hill. His black Mercedes sedan parked out front looked like it had been tagged with graffiti—until we discovered he'd done this to his own car. A few months later, he repainted his car *a la paint-by-numbers* into eight pink, yellow, green, and turquoise rectangles. We also heard a funny story about Flea from our next-door neighbor Al, an affable and disarmingly candid spirit who walked the hill with his wife every evening and two years earlier had bumped into Flea on the sidewalk:

Al: "Hi, I'm Al!"

Flea: "Hi, I'm Flea." Al gives Flea a friendly nudge on his shoulder.

Al: "C'mon, man! What kind of name is "Flea"? What's your real name?"

The international rock star was suddenly very, very human.

Flea: "Um…Mike."

But three houses below us on the corner was a massive structure that had been under construction since we arrived. Soon a black limousine with license plate "Voice 1" showed up—and that's when we discovered that this was the fortress of Don LaFontaine, the legendary "King of Voice-overs." Don was *the* voice of movie trailers and network promos. Not everyone knew his name, but *everyone* knew his voice. I had grown up wowed by his gripping sound in theaters during film previews—how he could move us emotionally—and thought he had the best job in the world. I had recently begun taking voice-over classes. So on a leisurely Saturday afternoon when I saw the limo parked outside, I decided to ramble over and introduce myself.

His house resembled Fort Knox—four stories of concrete, sixty yards wide, few if any windows, and a recessed entrance with two massive steel doors, every bit as impersonal as the façade. I summoned my courage and pressed the call button. A housekeeper answered sweetly, "Yes?" with just enough fall and rise in her tone to preserve my confidence.

"Hi, is Mr. LaFontaine there, please?" I chimed into the security box.

"Just a moment, please," she responded.

Ten seconds passed. Then, thundering through the speaker, came a deep, commanding voice: "HELLLL-OOOOOO??"

Hearing that rumble, I felt like a squeaky, prepubescent twelve-year-old: "Um, Mr. LaFontaine, hi…uh…my name is Kari Loya, and I…uh…I live just up the street here and…well…simply wanted to welcome you to the neighborhood… I'm also uh…interested in voice-overs and—"

Another crack of thunder stopped me. "VOICE OVERZZ?!"

I'd uttered the magic words. Suddenly, the vault opened and there stood the fifty-five-year-old Don LaFontaine with his dark bushy hair (ten years before appearing bald in the well-known Geico spot), OP cord shorts, Loony-Tunes t-shirt, gold chain, and burly chest hair shooting out to rival Burt Reynolds.

"HI! I'M DON," he bellowed as he extended his hand to shake mine. It's one thing to hear the "Voice of God" in a theater. It's quite another to stand two feet from God's mouth. And then, perhaps what every spiritual person on the planet hopes to hear: "C'MONNN IN!"

Don promptly invited me on a tour of his house. Our first stop was the theater—a huge room with a dropdown movie screen and a massive wrap around couch. Dolby Surround Sound speakers covered the walls.

"Check this out!" he said, like a ten-year-old with a new toy, popping a Dolby promotional disc into his brand-new laser disc player (this was 1995, before anyone owned DVDs or had surround sound systems in their home). A freight train appeared on the screen causing the entire room to tremble just like the big LA quake had six months earlier.

We continued down a hallway lined with photo after photo of Don with other celebrities. Displayed in the middle was a framed replica of his star on the Hollywood Walk of Fame, inscribed: "Don LaFontaine: The Voice of Hollywood."

The tour continued: massage and spa center, backyard patio and ionized pool with sweeping views of Burbank and Glendale, and so on. Who wouldn't love LA living here? We ended in the kitchen where, over a can of soda, Don shared how he had started doing voice-overs three decades earlier.

Had I been further along in my career, I would have peppered him with questions, but as someone just getting his feet wet, I held back. Yet what was clear was that Don LaFontaine loved his career with a passion, had spent countless hours—surely Malcolm Gladwell's ten thousand—to become the best at his craft, enjoyed a comfortable lifestyle with his family, and was enormously down to earth. He had even welcomed a complete stranger into his home.

Twelve years later I bumped into Don again, this time at an industry-related event in New York City. During the intermission, I walked over to reintroduce myself and thank him for taking time to meet with me years before in the Los Feliz Hills. I updated him on the progress I'd made in my career, praised him for his work in voicing the Academy Awards, and expressed my own hope of announcing the Oscars "perhaps in another ten years!"

A book signing followed the event and Don was one of a half-dozen celebrities penning his name, so I stuck around. But rather than have Don sign his book, I had brought along one of my voice-over demo CDs precisely for this occasion. I'd even scripted what I would have him write: "Kari, You're next. Don LaFontaine." But when I got to him, I hesitated. *Let him go,* I thought. *Let's see what he comes up with on his own.* Sure enough, he had already picked up on my ambition, and with his sense of humor and biting promo style, he threw down the gauntlet—like God toying with a mere mortal: "Kari, COME AND GET ME! Don LaFontaine." Genius. Thanks for the inspiration, Mr. LaFontaine.

End Note: Sadly, Don LaFontaine died September 1, 2008 after a remarkable career in which he voiced nearly five thousand movie trailers and hundreds of thousands of commercials and promos.

 Bonus Adventures: www.MyTop40at40.com
- *Watch the Geico spot with Don LaFontaine*
- *See autographed voice-over demo with Don's message*
- *Hear Kari's commentary*

9

The Industry's Little Secret
An inside tip from a Hollywood temp agency

Different cities assign different cachets to different professions. In New York, finance trumps all. The crowd at a cocktail party will inevitably gravitate to those working on Wall Street. In the Bay Area, Silicon Valley rules, although occasionally yielding to Save-the-World non-profits. But in Los Angeles, entertainment is king. Everyone refers to it as *The Industry*. You're a banker? Boooorrinnng. Software programmer? Yawwnn. Saving the seals? Party over. Wait—did you say you're an agent, producer, writer, actor, musician, or model? Then let's do lunch!

So when I needed short-term work in LA before moving to Brazil, I figured I should at least consider *The Industry*, particularly given my interest in voice-overs. A friend suggested I contact the Friedman Agency on Sunset Boulevard since they staffed a wide range of temp jobs for the Hollywood studios, from mailroom gophers to performers. She had landed an interesting gig several years before and was still friendly with the main placement executive. Without any particular job in mind, I decided to give it a whirl.

At the temp agency, I completed a battery of forms including a comprehensive inventory of skills and talents that made me feel grossly incompetent and uninteresting. Lesson-planning, problem-solving, presentation skills, and people-management—all gained through my work with Teach For America—were nowhere on the list, though "juggling fire" would have scored me some serious points. Next came the automated typing test. I was a decent typist, but had never stopped to measure my words-per-minute. Suddenly, I was strapped in at a computer like a NASCAR driver in pole position. When the sixty-second clock began, I launched a furious attack on the keyboard, prizing speed and power-of-key-stroke over accuracy.

Thirty minutes and various forms later, one of the proverbial post-college Hollywood assistants finally called my name for my formal interview and escorted me down the hall into a beautiful, spacious office overlooking the Sunset Strip and the Hollywood Hills. On the left was a stately desk, where the placement executive sat. After breaking the ice with conversation about our mutual friend, we chatted for twenty minutes about my background and interests. At one point in the conversation, she asked if I could answer two phones at once.

"Sure," I replied, not thinking much of the question.

"How about *three?*" she fired back.

"I think I could do anything!" I blurted out. This sounded bolder than I meant. What I wanted to say was, "I think I could do just about anything, *assuming it's a realistic goal and that I practice.*" After all, I had just finished three incredibly empowering years with Teach for America and, quite frankly, strongly believed—as I still do today—that if I set my mind toward accomplishing any realistic goal, I would indeed accomplish it, provided I was armed with patience and perseverance. But my über-confidence suddenly changed the course of our conversation.

"You're *very* cocky," she remarked slowly, still sizing me up as if she were appraising a sculpture, "...and I like that." She leaned back in her leather chair with her hands calmly folded in her lap while observing me keenly.

"For example," she noted, "just look at your posture."

Without realizing it, I was leaning forward in my chair with my arms propped on her desk, like a leopard ready to strike. She wasn't the least bit fazed, although now I was becoming self-conscious.

"But let me tell you something about Hollywood," she confided, the veteran slugger pulling the rookie batter aside for some advice. "There are two things that scare people in Hollywood: energy and intelligence."

Her point? The entertainment world was far from a meritocracy. Money, looks, and connections often mattered more than competence. How, she insinuated, might I respond if someone clearly unqualified was my boss—or even my boss's boss? How would I get along with everyone? How would I play the game? How would I manage *up*?

For better or worse, I didn't stick around to find out. Instead, I spent the next four months working at Adventure 16, an outdoor store, which pre-dated REI, on Olympic Boulevard in Westwood and the only retailer where I genuinely enjoyed shopping. It was a good experience, but I remember very little. Yet the wise counsel packed in *The Industry's Little Secret* I've never forgotten.

 Bonus Adventures: www.MyTop40at40.com
- *See and hear Kari's first voice-over cassette tape demo*
- *Hear Kari's commentary*

10

A Dream Called Rio
My search for soccer, samba, and soul

In June of 1998 I ran away to Rio de Janeiro for what I dubbed my *Graduate School of Life.* Just six months earlier, I had finished an empowering three-year stint with Teach for America. My confidence and sense of adventure were soaring and *carpediem* was my modus operandi. *What next?* was the big question. I had briefly considered the well-trammeled paths of consulting or grad school, but when I thought deeply about it, one simple dream stood out: I wanted to play soccer on the beaches of Rio.

My infatuation with Brazilian soccer began in high school. Long before the internet and the hundreds of cable channels, the only way I could watch soccer—other than the weekly "Soccer Made In Germany" broadcasts on PBS—was to rent video tapes through a store in St. Louis, the hotbed of American soccer at the time. The first videos I received were by Weil Coerver and showed mechanical and precise movements, German football at its scientific and disciplined best. But then I discovered "Pele: The Master and his Method," where Pele and a handful of players, including kids, scampered barefoot to a gentle samba rhythm along the beach in a pick-up game. Everyone was laughing. And everyone was an artist in this improvisational dance. I was smitten.

My passion for *futebol* extended after college to all things Brazilian: the electrifying batucadas and kaleidoscopic colors of the *escolas de samba* during Carnaval; the sensuous and sultry sounds of bossa nova, reminding you that a conversation in Brazil starts not with "What do you do?" but "Who is your girlfriend?"; the refreshing mix of lime, sugar, and *cachaça* for a *caipirinha,* and a beer on a hot day served *estupidamente gelada*—stupidly ice-cold; the never-ending *rodizios* in the *churrasquerias*, God's gift to carnivores; and, of course, the graceful girls—*garotas*—of Ipanema on every other corner, who, no matter their shape or size, sway with supreme confidence as if from birth they've been told "You are beautiful."

Finally, the language. Many think Italian is the most beautiful language in the world, but for me it's Brazilian Portuguese, specifically the Carioca accent in Rio. It's Italian *after* a day at the beach—with no drama of work, family, or finances. At all hours of the day, the music of the language communicates, "Relax, everything will work out just fine." In fact, my favorite word in Portuguese is *ginga*, a term I once saw defined as "The graceful swaying of the hips of the mulata samba dancer and the Brazilian football player." Talk about packing a punch. In short, it's that wonderfully creative, go-with-the-flow spirit that defines the Brazilian way of life.

Then the sounds. While a Paulistano (from Sao Paulo) will call a door a "POR-ta" with a trilled "r," a Carioca turns the "r" to an "h" and says "POHHHHH-ta," blowing softly in your ear. The final "s" on words becomes "shhhh," turning ordinary conversation into a hushed romantic encounter. And the "t" and "d," when followed by "i" or "e", become a provocative "ch" and "zh," like the sexy slurring of words after two glasses of wine. But the coup de grace? Rio's double meaning—not only does it mean "river," it also means "I laugh."

At twenty-six, I brimmed with confidence that I could set and accomplish goals as well as anyone, but those Brazilians… those Brazilians were always smiling and laughing! What did they know that I didn't? I simply had to go to find out for myself.

Two other key ideas framed my trip. First, a friend of my dad's had given his kids a one-way ticket anywhere in the world as a graduation present. This was brilliant—a gift of exploration, creativity, and resourcefulness. After all, how the hell will you get home? On that note, I bought myself a one-way ticket to Rio. Second, an anthropologist I knew explained that the minimum timeframe to break free from existing paradigms—and not only see new things but see the same things differently through a new lens—was twelve months. I resolved to find a way to stay in Brazil for eighteen months.

While nighttime dreams magically make sense, daytime dreams—our real goals and ambitions—require a lot of good ol' fashioned hard work. To realize my romantic vision of playing soccer on the beaches of Rio, I needed to overcome two major obstacles: 1) My tourist visa would allow me to stay only three months, renewable once; and 2) My savings of fifteen hundred dollars would last just six weeks. So I needed a work visa, and I needed a job. I also needed friends—I knew no one except for a friend of a friend who agreed to pick me up at the airport—and I needed to learn Portuguese. Fast.

I pounded the pavement hard in three specific directions and everything started to fall into place. First, after four weeks, I landed a full-time position at one of the largest language schools in Brazil teaching English and Spanish to teens and adults. Not only did that give me a basic income, the company agreed to sponsor my work visa. Second, I drummed up voice-over work in English and Spanish at a number of recording studios around the city. Seventeen months later, just before returning to the States, I proudly welcomed all air travelers to the country: "Welcome to Brazil!" my voice rang out, before reminding them to shop duty-free. Third, I played a complete wildcard—becoming a model—and ended up scoring several on-camera gigs and a few minutes of fame.* In short, I survived my *Graduate School of Life* and all the ups, downs, and

---

* Andy Warhol never mentioned that our fifteen minutes of fame might come *outside* the borders of the United States. For one of my on-camera projects—a major national commercial—I appeared as the American engineer who had designed the new water ride for *Terra Encantada*, the project of Brazilian model-singer-host Xuxa. Terra Encantada was billed as the largest theme park in Latin America at the time. The commercial was a funny spot in which I began explaining the technology behind the ride only to be swept by a wave downriver mid-sentence. Weeks later when the commercial finally aired, students at the language school literally popped out of their classrooms to peer, point, and whisper when I arrived. Vendors in the nearby markets and shops would also murmur, smile, and point in my direction. But my favorite moment came a few days later when I travelled to the language school's corporate headquarters for my weekly visit. I entered the building and greeted the main security guard at the front reception. His eyes beamed and his smile widened even more than usual. I knew what was coming, or at least I thought I did.

"Hey!" he shouted back, "I didn't know you were an engineer!"

exams it threw at me. And yes, I spent many, many days living my dream of playing soccer on the beaches of Rio. But ironically, one of the biggest lessons came before I even left the United States.

I hadn't known the first thing about modeling so I literally bought a book called *How to Become a Model*, weeks before moving to Brazil. It turned out I needed a portfolio. As luck would have it, my sister had just graduated from Parson's School of Design in New York, majoring in Photography, and would overlap with me in Eugene before I left for Brazil, so she agreed to help me. Over two weeks and on a shoestring budget, we completed my portfolio—we scoured the city for backdrops and raided the malls for outfits which we returned the next day because "they didn't quite fit." Assembling the portfolio also meant wearing make-up for the first time and shaving my chest, which made me feel like I'd lost my testosterone. But what surprised me most was how, just a week into the photo shoot, I found myself worrying about physical blemishes I'd never even noticed before—a tiny pimple, a wrinkle, a chipped tooth…the list went on and on and every day I fretted about more of these "imperfections." It was easy to see how on-camera work could play with your head and drive you crazy. I realized I never wanted my financial situation or self-worth to depend on my looks.

Bonus Adventures: www.MyTop40at40.com
- *See Kari's model portfolio*
- *Watch Terra Encantada commercial*
- *Watch Kari's beach interview about futebol in the BBC documentary "A Whole New Ball Game"*
- *Read* How to be a Carioca *(Priscilla Ann Goslin)*
- *Hear Kari's commentary*

PART THREE
Age 26-30

11

Losing My Speedo Virginity
Crossing a cultural threshold

Walk any two blocks in downtown Buenos Aires and you'll likely pass a bookstore, a café, and a tie shop. But stroll down any two blocks in the Zona Sul of Rio—the fashionable neighborhoods including Ipanema and Leblon—and you'll notice a gym, a juice bar, and a swimsuit shop displaying tiny bikinis and *sungas,* the Brazilian word for Speedos. Life in Rio revolves around the beach. The Brazilian equivalent of "It's not my cup of tea" is "It's not my beach"—*Não é a minha praia.* That implies that you do have *some* beach—everyone has a beach.

And that means lots of Speedos coming and going: Speedos at poolside barbecues; Speedos on motorcycles, miles from the water; Speedos next to suits and ties at juice bars; and, of course, Speedos at the beach itself. Speedos everywhere.

The only time growing up that I had ever spotted a Speedo was on swimmers. The skimpy jewel-protectors always provoked a flurry of giggles among most kids and even adults, at least those whose kids weren't on the swim team. Speedos *in the wild*—those outside formal swimming competitions—were nearly non-existent. You might occasionally glimpse a television or film clip of those crazy Europeans on the French Riviera. You might also come across someone buzzing on bud strolling through the crowd at the Oregon County Fair in a turquoise thong alongside a companion sporting a parrot on their shoulder, but these were clearly exceptions—and folks you really didn't want to be around. So when I moved to Rio—Land of the *Sunga*—I knew that sooner or later I'd have to face my prudishness head on.

I finally capitulated after six months and joined the party in Buzios, a rustic beach town one hundred miles north of Rio. At my girlfriend's urging, I entered a bathing suit boutique along the cobblestone *Rua das Pedras* and agreed to try on a *sunga*. I browsed the selection and settled on a conservative choice: black with two white stripes down the sides. This at least would be like walking carefully into the ocean up to my knees, then my waist, slowly splashing my arms and chest, before finally submerging myself. Bright red, yellow, blue, or green would have been a screaming dive straight into the water—and I wasn't yet emotionally ready for that commitment.

I stepped into the dressing room with the flimsy piece of fabric in my hand. I wondered how on earth something so tiny—a stark contrast from boxers or Patagonia baggies—could conceal everything. It was like being given a bow to wrap a birthday present but wondering *where the hell's the wrapping paper?* I disrobed, then hoisted up the bathing suit to my waist, disregarding thoughts about hygiene and how many other customers had tried on the same suit. I cinched the drawstrings and tugged the sides upward. Then I stretched the leg part downward. Again upward, again downward, back up and back down. But after sixty seconds I realized this neurotic tug-of-war was all in vain—I'd already attained maximum coverage. With my voice nearly cracking, I whispered through the dressing room doors, "Do you, um… have a bigger size?"

Hearing nothing but silence, I crept out of the dressing room onto the store floor where both my girlfriend and the smiling shop lady zeroed in on my groin. The latter quickly approached me. *Pat. Pat. Pat. Squeeze. Squeeze. Pinch. Pinch. Tug. Tug. Tug.* Her hands ran around my loins as if she were kneading pizza dough. "*Tá joia!*—It fits perfectly!" she assured me cheerfully, after the no-shame pat down for which many guys would have dropped a few bills. Feeling somewhere between a kid sporting new sneakers and a kid called to the principal's office, I simply smiled at my new self in the mirror, tossed my other shorts in the store bag, and exited the shop. I was a Speedo-virgin no more.

 BONUS ADVENTURES: www.MyTop40at40.com
- *See Kellogg MBAs after losing their speedo virginity*
- *See Kari's holiday card from Ipanema*
- *Hear Kari's commentary*

12

Prisoner at Alcatraz
A piercing response from a former inmate

The most well-known prison in the world is Alcatraz. It hasn't functioned as a prison for decades, but every year it draws tourists from around the world eager to explore "The Rock" and learn more about its fabled history. Tourism has reached such heights that an "Escape from Alcatraz Triathlon" was created where athletes could attempt what no prisoners ever accomplished—swim off "The Rock" through the fog and frigid, shark-infested currents to the mainland, then continue their "escape" on bike and foot.

I finally had the chance to visit Alcatraz in 1996 and opted, perhaps uncharacteristically, for the easy path—the guided tour. We wandered through the narrow cells, peered into the solitary confinement chamber, and listened to tales of Al Capone, the Birdman, and other legendary convicts. The most hardened, dangerous, and incorrigible men in America had called this place home.

In the last room at the end of the tour, a gray-haired, grandfatherly gentleman of average stature held court from behind a table. This clean-shaven, well-dressed man, it turned out, was a former inmate, a convict, who had returned to sign copies of his book about his years on "The Rock." The choreography of his dancing white eyebrows, warm holiday smile, and lively stories captivated everyone, like Santa regaling saucer-eyed children with tales from the North Pole.

And that's when I chimed in: "How were you different when you got out of Alcatraz from when you arrived?" I'd always wondered about the ability of the penal system to rehabilitate as well as to punish—could someone really come out a more law-abiding, productive citizen? The genial raconteur extinguished all warmth from his face and glared directly at me, oblivious now to everyone else in the room.

"Whennn I lllleft Aaalcatraz…" he began, dragging each word through the dark, murky recesses of his memory, "I wwwwas one…mmmmmean…ssson-of-a-bitch…" He had nothing to hide and continued his raw, hardened reflection: "And I…wwwould…have…done…AAANYTHING…" Here he paused, lifted his hand, and pointed his wizened finger at my chest, "… including take YYYOUR life…NNNOT to go back."

The crowd blanched and there was an awkward silence. I thanked him politely…and left the building.

 BONUS ADVENTURES: www.MyTop40at40.com
- *Hear Kari's commentary*
- *Visit www.escapefromalcatraztriathlon.com*

13

Top Gunning in DC
An unexpected thrill flying commercial

In one of the great scenes from the classic movie *Top Gun,* Maverick, the aptly-named pilot played by Tom Cruise, breaks the sacred rule of the military base and "buzzes the tower"—that is, he flies low and fast across the runway without actually landing, riling the cantankerous commander. On a commercial flight into DC's National Airport in the late nineties, I unexpectedly got a mini-taste of what Maverick might have felt.

Shortly after our 737 took off from Denver, the pilot welcomed us aboard with that comforting monotone that invites everyone to close their eyes and go to sleep: *Everything is completely under control* (there's a reason Richard Simmons never became a pilot).

But if you were paying close attention, you would have heard, "Folks, some of you may have noticed that minor explosion on take-off…" *Explosion*—not a word you want to hear anywhere, let alone on an airplane. My ears perked up.

"It appears that we may have popped our front tire…" the voice continued. "We'll see what we can do to assess the situation…and we'll give you an update as we get closer to DC." In other words, "Houston, we have a problem."

But commercial pilots must surely spend as much time practicing vocal delivery as honing their flight skills so that phrases like "minor explosion on take-off" are no more alarming then "sixty-five degrees and sunny in Washington." So I fell asleep.

Three hours later as we approached DC, the pilot returned to the intercom, casually explaining "for those who may have missed the earlier announcement" that our front tires may have been punctured. The only way to confirm this would be to fly by the control tower and allow a team of experts to have a look. None of us were sure what exactly this meant, but *everything seemed to be under control*—his steady tone reassured us. In addition, the pilot informed us that all flights into and out of National Airport had been suspended and that we should now prepare for "landing." Everyone, including the flight attendants, took their seats, the landing gear hummed as it lowered, and within ninety seconds we were descending abruptly toward the runway. But rather than land, we leveled out just fifteen feet above the ground and continued flying at that height across the entire runway, literally buzzing the tower. As we neared the end of the runway after this unique view of the airport, we shot back upwards like a normal take-off.

Everyone sat quietly, eagerly awaiting the next words from our captain, like patients desperate to hear their medical test results. After two…very…long…minutes, the pilot reported that indeed our front two tires were punctured. Murmurs and whispers broke out through the cabin as everyone began speculating with their neighbor what this meant—*and how the hell we would land.*

Yet once again the pilot's measured tone and fluency in euphemisms soothed us all. We would be landing shortly with a "modified technique" where he would land on the back wheels, reduce our speed as much as possible, then drop the nose at the last minute. In other words, we had just buzzed the tower, and now we were going to pop an airplane wheelie! This was quickly becoming a teenage boy's dream flight. Finally, the pilot added, "When we land, there will be some…'equipment'…on the runway. This is simply… 'standard procedure'…Please prepare for landing."

Everyone went silent. We banked a hard left and descended once more. Only this time, dozens of phosphorescent yellow fire trucks lined both sides of the track as far as we could see. We touched down on our back wheels and bolted forward, holding our nose up at a thirty-degree angle through the blur of yellow emergency vehicles. Twenty degrees…fifteen degrees…ten…five…and still…not a single…breath among… the passengers…and finally…SCREECHHHHHHH!!! Our nose touched down and we continued forward. But no smoke…and no fire! We slowed, then stopped. Everyone let out an enormous sigh of relief, then applauded our new hero, the pilot, and his textbook poise under pressure. We were all fine. Better than fine, in fact. After all, for fifteen minutes, we'd each experienced the rare thrill of being Top Gun.

 Bonus Adventures: www.MyTop40at40.com

- *Hear Kari's commentary*

14

Some Soup with Sumos
An unusual training center in Tokyo

The first time I ever stood face-to-face with a sumo wrestler—or face-to-belly, to be more accurate—I had the same anxious thought that must have crossed the blonde Ann Darrow's mind when she was sacrificially offered up to King Kong: *Will he crush me or won't he?* My heart skipped a beat while I awaited his decision. Fortunately, the ponytailed giant bowed reverently, stepped aside, and politely waved us into his home.

It wasn't really just his home. He, in fact, shared it with nineteen other sumo wrestlers. After all, this was a sumo boarding and training facility, located in a non-descript residential neighborhood of Tokyo and run by a former sumo Grandmaster. We had received a rare invitation to this sanctuary for lunch via my sister who was teaching English in Japan at the time and had befriended the Grandmaster's business partners. Imagine if Kobe and his Laker buddies lived and trained together—and you were the lucky, random foreign tourist picked to watch their practice then have lunch with them. This felt like a Japanese version of that.

We'd already had a blast since arriving in Japan a week earlier. My sister had whisked my mom and me through a slew of quintessential tourist experiences: zooming across Honshu Island at lightning speeds on the *Shinkansen* bullet train; squeezing into "Manhattan-seems-empty" rush-hour subway cars in Tokyo while dapper, uniformed attendants with hats and white gloves delicately pushed us inside like sardines before the doors closed; cruising trendy Shinjuku and gawking at the twelve-inch platform shoes in every hue of neon on Japanese teenyboppers; picnicking—shoeless, of course—with locals *en masse* at a *sakura* (cherry blossom) festival whose beauty arouses even greater passion than autumn foliage among New Englanders; and sampling the novelty of conveyor-belt sushi between swills of Sapporo and sake. *Shinkansen*, *subways*, *shoes*, *sakura*, *sushi*, *Sapporo*, and *sake*—we'd nearly completed our alliterative journey through Japan. Now we'd secured one final "S" experience: Sumos.

After passing through the front entry and doffing our shoes, we followed our six-foot, three-hundred-pound robed host through a labyrinth of sliding wooden doors into a backroom measuring approximately forty-by-forty feet, divided into two sections. On the near side was a normal wooden floor extending out ten feet, neatly covered with tatami mats. The remaining thirty-by-forty foot space was a sunken dirt floor that ran wall-to-wall. The dirt, clay, and sand combination had been elegantly groomed like the infield of a Major League ballpark.

Our guide gestured for us to take a seat on the mats, then returned to offer us tea. The giant stretched his tree trunk arms and baseball mitt hands toward us while clasping a dainty porcelain cup of green tea, scarcely bigger than a thimble. Every step of his caused the floor to tremble, yet this same giant sumo wrestler was also the consummate graceful waiter.

Minutes later, the other residents of the sumo stable arrived. Eighteen *rikishi*—literally, strong men—replete with ponytails and wearing nothing but their *mawashi*—those oversized, padded jockstraps—proceeded onto the dirt floor and stood in five rows facing us. Everyone weighed between two hundred twenty and three hundred fifty pounds, but the guys just over two bills seemed remarkably scrawny in this context, like prepubescent seventh graders next to high school seniors. For the next ninety minutes, we witnessed an intense workout of lateral leg lifts, windmill slaps, bear hugs, and a king-of-the-mountain sumo battle where the winner remained in the ring until he ran out of gas and was dislodged by a new king who repeated the cycle.

But what I remember most about the workout were the grunts and the sweat. The grunts I expected. Like a ferocious backhand, an Olympic clean-and-jerk, or a Lawrence Taylor hit—who wouldn't grunt if you collided with a three hundred pound boulder barreling in the other direction? But the sweat…I've never seen anything like it in my life. Thirty minutes into the workout, streams—literally *streams* of sweat—ran off the fleshy mountains onto the ground forming puddles. By the end of the workout, the puddles were lakes.

Several of the biggest wrestlers looked as if they had tubes connected to their body, like a parody on *Saturday Night Live*, shooting liquid in different directions, all less than ten feet in front of us. They'd become human waterslides.

While we watched eighteen of the fighters grapple, grind, bump, and sweat, we could also see two of the sumos, including the one who had greeted us at the door and served us tea, chopping, stirring, and pouring off in a corner kitchen. In rotation two of the wrestlers would take the day off from their physical regimen to focus exclusively on domestic duties and prepare the meals for the rest of the athletes. It seems that cooking, cleaning, and serving were just as important to their training as fighting.

When the wrestlers finished their workout and left the pit to shower, the two on kitchen duty served us lunch. We remained on the tatami mats, but sat in a small circle. Our hosts then placed in the middle a huge pot of *chanko nabe*, the hearty staple stew of the sumos, and put place settings down for each of us. Though our portions may have been drastically different, this same meal would be served minutes later to Japan's next crop of national heroes. It was a wonderful treat.

Never give a sword to a man who can't dance, goes the refrain. Or perhaps cook, clean, and serve. This group of modern warriors was mastering *all aspects* of the ancient art of sumo in the *Land of the Rising Sun*.

 Bonus Adventures: www.MyTop40at40.com

- *See sumo training facility*
- *See Japan trip slideshow*
- *Hear Kari's commentary*

15

Two Words
Priceless advice from the president

I n my second grade class at the Edison Brentwood Academy in East Palo Alto was a student named Ulysses. Despite his imposing name, Ulysses was ten pounds lighter and stood four inches shorter than just about everyone else in the class, including the girls. His name also belied his soft-spoken nature and *Leave-it-to-Beaver* face. Rather than a determined leader, Ulysses was routinely the caboose of our train of students when we walked around campus—and easily distracted, he just as often fell off the train completely. But Ulysses' wonderful spark was that he always seemed to have a tale to weave.

Most of the time this was related to his homework. I'd ask him why he hadn't completed his assignment and his face would go blank, his tongue would protrude slightly from his sealed lips, and his eyes would squint as he looked off to the side, trying to remember the facts correctly while simultaneously trying to decide which facts to omit, embellish, or invent altogether.

So when we returned from spring break in April of 2000 and Ulysses, in his broken English, announced that he'd met President Bill Clinton over the vacation, I simply smiled and played along: "That's great, Ulysses! How did you manage that?" He proceeded to spin his story.

When President Clinton came to East Palo Alto (I was unaware at the time that Clinton had even visited), Ulysses had gone to the main street with his older brother to catch a glimpse of the president. They watched from afar as President Clinton descended from the motorcade and began walking in the street, greeting the throngs behind the police tape. But then their view became blocked, so Ulysses—smiling proudly as he recalled this part—used both his wiles and size to his advantage. He began skirting around and even between the legs of onlookers, working his way to the police tape. After just a few minutes, Ulysses found himself at the front of the crowd.

"And there were these two men with sunglasses and something hanging out of their ears," Ulysses gestured excitedly, an eight-year-old's interpretation of Secret Service agents.

"And then what happened?" I inquired, now more intrigued.

"President Clinton came and shook my hand and told me to learn lots. He even wrote me a note!" Ulysses was a gifted storyteller, but this was a stretch even for him. I still didn't know whether or not to believe him. I smiled, thanked him for sharing his great story, and invited him to bring the note to class.

Sure enough, the next day Ulysses arrived at school first thing in the morning along with everyone else, only this time he wasn't the quiet caboose on the train, but the mighty engine. Before he'd even entered the classroom, he reached into his pocket, pulled out his fist, and revealed the contents— exactly what you might expect from the pocket of an eight-year-old: candy wrappers, crumbs, a broken crayon, and a small folded white slip of paper. With his other hand, he quickly grasped the white slip of paper and handed it to me, beaming with pride, like a kid waiting to blow out his birthday candles. On the inside of the paper was a simple, handwritten message in black ink: "To Ulysses, Learn lots! Bill Clinton." Touché, Ulysses. And congratulations, President Clinton. I can't imagine a more meaningful way to inspire a kid with just two words.

 BONUS ADVENTURES: www.MyTop40at40.com
- *Watch Kari's interview about The Edison Project on the PBS News Hour*
- *Hear Kari's commentary*

16

Why the Tarantula Crossed the Road
Those sexy Bay Area spiders

The San Francisco Bay Area has some of the best cycling in the world. You can pedal through redwood
forests on Old La Honda Road near the heart of venture
capital; climb Mt. Tam for its panoramic views then swoop
down to the fog-enshrouded Stinson Beach for coffee;
cruise along Highway 1 near Half Moon Bay overlooking
the Pacific; or navigate the hilly streets of the City* before
crossing the majestic Golden Gate Bridge. And let's not

---

* San Francisco and New York City are the two places where residents,
when asked where they live by anyone in the general area, respond simply, "The City." San Franciscans will use "The City" as far away as seven
or eight towns; New Yorkers, God love 'em, use the term as far away as
seven or eight *states*. I still remember asking classmates at Dartmouth
where they were from. "*The* City," they replied casually. *What freakin' city
are you talking about? Manchester? Boston?* I still chuckle at that impressive
self-absorption.

forget the nearby vineyards of Napa, the mountains of Lake Tahoe, or the cliffs of Big Sur. But my most memorable ride—hands down, literally—was up to the 3,849 foot peak of Mt. Diablo near Walnut Creek, just east of the Bay.

Thirty minutes into the lung-busting climb, I passed what looked like a worn leather glove on the pavement and simply assumed that it had fallen from a gardener's pick-up truck, the way you sometimes see a random boot or umbrella along the road. Two hundred yards further I spotted another "glove," but as I rode closer, this looked like something different: roadkill. Only this wasn't your ordinary raccoon or porcupine—it looked more like a giant spider. Like a tarantula!

What the hell would a tarantula be doing in the Bay Area? I'd come across tarantulas in the Guatemalan jungles and the Amazon rainforest and knew they inhabited the American Southwest, but Northern California? It seemed right up there with spotting a penguin. I pedaled upwards while pondering this wildlife anomaly. Then, just ahead on the road, there it was: another tarantula, only this time a live one crawling across the pavement. I got off my bike just to witness this three-minute show—after all, how many people can say they've watched a tarantula cross the road?

One tarantula was weird. Two? Creepy. But in the next five minutes when I saw the third and fourth, I totally freaked out and nearly called 9-1-1 to report the arachnid invasion. Adrenaline shot me toward the summit at a record pace, where I saw another cyclist starting down.

"Dude, did you see all those fucking tarantulas?" I shouted with panic-propelled profanity.

"Yeah," he replied nonchalantly, "The park ranger says there are quite a few around now. Says it's mating season. He even picked one up off the ground."

Now *that* got my attention. I had always thought that tarantulas were the soft, fuzzy, eight-legged equivalent of a Great White and once they locked in on you, you were doomed. Maybe I'd been duped by Hollywood imagery, but I was still amazed that the ranger had actually held one in his hands.

"For real?" I asked incredulously.

"Yeah, man," he confirmed with a surfer's cool, "It was pretty sweet."

Reassured that this September spider migration was normal, I swilled my Gatorade, relished the sweeping views of Half-Dome to the east and the Bay to the west, then began coasting down. After about a half mile, a small, dark figure was crossing the road ahead—another male tarantula in search of companionship. I braked, then got off my bike: it was just me and Mr. Hairy Tarantula.

Bungee jumping, spelunking, white-water rafting—they'd all given me the liberating experience of a good scare at earlier points in my life. And now, confident I wouldn't die, I was about to test another way. I stretched my palm and five fingers on the ground six inches in front of the creature. My pulse quickened as the gap between giant spider and soft fleshy hand narrowed. Six inches…four inches…

two inches…*gulp*. Without breaking stride, my furry friend tangoed and tickled his way over my hand while I held my breath—then continued his innocuous journey to the other side of the road.

By the time I descended the mountain and returned to my car, I'd seen nine live tarantulas and seven roadkills, a one-of-a-kind athletic tally. But more importantly, I now understood *why the tarantula crossed the road*: to get a little lovin'!

 Bonus Adventures: www.MyTop40at40.com
- *See Team Dartmouth Wine-to-Waves (Calistoga to Santa Cruz) running relay poster*
- *Hear Kari's commentary*

17

A Test to See What You're Made Of
Thoughts from Ironman New Zealand

wo nights before competing in the 2001 New Zealand Ironman Triathlon in Lake Taupo, all the athletes were invited along with their families to participate in an international goodwill parade, watch a Huka Warrior dance, and eat to our hearts content at a pasta dinner. The celebrity keynote speaker was John Collins, founder of the original Ironman Triathlon in Hawaii in 1978 involving just fifteen men, or perhaps, brash guinea pigs. John planned to compete in the Lake Taupo event himself—his first race outside Hawaii—and his wife and daughter had signed up as well. We all wondered what the inventor of this masochistic global movement would say.

As John stepped to the podium to deliver his remarks, his warm smile, thin frame, and silver hair could have marked him as a pastor reminding his congregation of an upcoming pancake breakfast. Instead, this guy's guy explained how he had concocted the seemingly crazy Ironman triathlon: "A few military buddies and I were sitting around over some beers in Oahu one night trying to determine who was the best athlete, who was the toughest. After much heated debate, we finally settled on combining the Oahu big three: the 2.4-mile Waikiki Roughwater Swim, the 112-mile Around-Oahu Bike Race, and the 26.2-mile Honolulu Marathon. This endurance event, we agreed, would be the ultimate test to see what you were made of."

After his address, I approached John, thanked him for his remarks, then asked him what in his life had been the greatest tests to see what *he* was made of. Without missing a beat, he answered, "The first Ironman. Quite frankly, we didn't know what was going to happen." In other words, *was it humanly possible? Might someone die?* It made sense. Nowadays, completing an Ironman is still a remarkable accomplishment, but the mystery is largely gone. The road has been scientifically-paved with hundreds of books, carefully-calibrated electrolyte liquids and protein bars, and specialized gear for every minute of the pre-race, post-race, and the race itself. It's the difference between scaling Everest now—still an incredible feat—and climbing alongside Hillary and Norgay in 1953. The real challenge—and for many the thrill—is plunging headfirst into the unknown. My follow up question helped put this in perspective.

"What about the *second* greatest test?" I asked. He paused to reflect while gazing at the floor. Then, when it was clear he had weighed through several possibilities, he looked at me squarely and replied, "It was 1962 during the Cuban Missile Crisis. I was serving in the Navy aboard a nuclear submarine off the coast of Siberia. For four days straight, we were being hunted by a Russian nuclear sub. I stood watch through the night."

My own motives to compete in an Ironman arose three decades earlier when I'd watched, transfixed, as Julie Moss staggered and crawled the last mile of the marathon to cross the finish of the Hawaiian Ironman in second place. Julie's performance—the epitome of a conscious choice to push beyond your limits and lay it all on the line in pursuit of a goal—inspired millions, including me, to do the same.

I was an athletic (read: "hyperactive") twelve-year-old at the time and was thrilled when the first recreational triathlons appeared: endurance training gave me a constructive place to channel excess energy and calm down.* The 1983 YMCA Triathlon in Eugene, Oregon—Track Capital USA and the birthplace of Nike—featured what is now commonly known as "Olympic" distances: a one-mile swim, a twenty-five-mile bike ride, and a six-point-two mile run. My dad competed alongside me the entire race—an early lesson in fatherhood—including our last-place exit from the open-water swim, which I did sidestroke due to my water phobia at the time.

---

* Long before ADHD entered our vernacular, I once had a teacher pull me aside after class because of my hyperactivity and say, "I've seen behavior like this before—and drugs were always involved!" The irony is that now drugs *are* involved—as the prescribed solution.

But we finished the triathlon with big smiles and participated in a couple more separately over the next two years. And although I drifted away from triathlons for nearly two decades, I never forgot my dream of competing in an Ironman. So, when fitness level, motivation, and time to train aligned in 2000, I decided to pull the trigger: Ironman New Zealand, the second oldest after Kona (originally Oahu). My dad once again joined me on the journey, this time as a spectator and support crew.

The Ironman, as John Collins had stated, was indeed a test. When I crossed the finish line in ten hours twenty-one minutes and change—a respectable first-crack, albeit thirty minutes shy of qualifying for Hawaii—I realized the main test had been the previous six months of training: five thirty outdoor swims in the cold morning rain, ten-mile runs through fog and darkness at the end of a long work day, even a solo nine-hour ride on Super Bowl Sunday. That kind of discipline and sense of sacrifice and purpose, though, are powerful elixirs, so much so that the race itself became a party. Well, a really painful party.

But what most blew my mind at Lake Taupo—and gives me goosebumps just writing about it—were the other racers who could have been the local Girl Scout den mother, the postal carrier, the supermarket clerk. Folks who looked like they had no business being out there and yet after fifteen-plus hours they were still battling, giving everything they had, knowing that "just finishing is a victory." Now *that* was inspiring. Everyone who crosses that finish line indeed earns bragging rights for life.

Bonus Adventures: www.MyTop40at40.com

- *See Kari with John Collins*
- *See Ironman New Zealand vs. Pamplona comparison*
- *Hear Kari's commentary*

18

Don't Drop the Pig!
One helluva party

I love a great party. The best parties mix familiar faces with new blood, provide some sort of educational and entertaining experience, and always include good eats and liberally-flowing libations. The first holiday soiree my roommates and I threw for Teach For America corps members at our pad in the Hollywood Hills in 1993 set a high bar. The jungle party our same crew threw the following year was even better. But my favorite bash, aside from my wedding, was the Ironman pig roast celebration I hosted in 2001 shortly after completing the New Zealand Ironman triathlon.

I had discovered that a sizable Tongan population resided in the Bay Area where I was teaching, and that when it came to pig roasts, these Pacific Islanders were pros—they roasted pigs like we grilled burgers. They even possessed a special permit from San Mateo County to build open pit fires in their backyards. Who knew? As luck would have it, one of my students was Tongan and his family offered to help. They simply asked how many guests I'd be feeding to determine the size of the pig, agreed to handle the entire roast, and told me to pick up the pig an hour before the party.

The first part of the evening's program was the premier of a fifteen-minute film chronicling my Ironman adventure in our makeshift Kodak Theater on two massive seventy-two-inch screens, which in pre-flat screen days resembled tanks. The film received rave reviews, but the *pièce de résistance* was our "Ironman simulation."

First, when guests approached our front door, the Hans Zimmer score from "Gladiator" blared out of a ghetto blaster tucked behind the bushes, transporting everyone to a battlefield. A list on the door matched the name of every "racer" with a number, which they branded onto their bicep and calf using a black marker. Then, courtesy of some creative computer programming by my techie roommate, they also donned a barcode bracelet corresponding to the same race number.

That was just the start. A good buddy who worked in my hometown for the largest provider of retail handheld scanners in the country had driven down with a top-of-the-line scanner. As each guest stepped inside the door, we scanned their bracelet. Their name immediately appeared on two computer monitors as part of a three-column webpage. The left column represented the 2.4-mile swim, the middle column the 112-mile bike, and the final column the 26.2-mile run. The gun had gone off!

Every time a racer put away a drink, either a cocktail or from the keg, they scanned themselves and posted a time next to their name. As soon as someone had scanned themselves twice, a final time was posted for the swim and their name advanced to the bike column. Four more drinks and they transitioned to the run. Drinks seven, eight, nine, and ten completed the marathon—and the race.

Only four of our fifty guests finished the course. The winner was a fiercely competitive Kiwi Olympic cyclist—a sprinter in the velodrome—a six-foot-five-inch oak tree who kept hitting his head on our chandelier. At one point in the evening, he had glanced at the monitor to view the standings and realized that he was only in second place. With Olympic resolution and efficiency, he took one long stride to the keg to fill his cup, pounded the beer, scanned himself, pivoted back to the keg, chugged another beer, scanned himself again, then studied the monitor with a smile. He had regained the lead.

Of course, he was also wobbling by the end of the party. And a six-foot-five-inch frame filled with liquid courage is a *lot* of courage. Our champion celebrated his victory by moving in on what remained of the pig, cracking open the skull, and feasting on its brains, *Lord of the Flies*-style. The three other finishers, yours truly included, followed suit—pumped like football fans rushing the field after a huge triumph, yet simultaneously puzzled like lemmings who just stepped off the cliff. The sheep brain I'd sampled in a Madrid tapas bar years earlier suddenly seemed pedestrian. And so ended the dramatic festivities.

But what had impressed me most occurred earlier that afternoon when I had swung by my Tongan student's home to say hello and see how the pig was coming along. As expected, the open pit fire blazed in the middle of their backyard. What totally surprised me, though, was a nine-foot steel steering wheel rod, propped a couple feet off the ground, skewering the pig over the coals. And on one end, behind the actual steering wheel, sat the grandfather ten inches off the ground on a comfortable, upholstered car seat *driving* the pig, just as naturally as he might play cards or watch baseball. The sort of thing MacGyver might rig up in the South Pacific.

When the grandfather left his post to grab a drink, the five kids who had been playing in the backyard all scurried to take his place, fighting over who would now occupy the seat and drive the pig. As they wrestled with each other and the wheel, rotating it brusquely back and forth, their mom scolded them in Tongan through the open kitchen window: *"O wa'eto Pu'aka! O wa'eto Pu'aka!"* *Don't drop the pig! Don't drop the pig!* Great advice. I loved it so much I designed a t-shirt with that on the front, my chief memento from an original party.

---

* I also love the Tongan word for "ten." The numbers "one" through "nine" are like the winding of the jack-in-the-box…*taha, ua, tolu, fa, nima, ono, fitu, valu, hiva*…and then, suddenly, the smiling jack bursts out waving his hands and shouts: *"HONGOFULU*!!"

 Bonus Adventures: www.MyTop40at40.com
- *See pig roast party*
- *Watch Kari's Ironman New Zealand film*
- *Hear Kari's commentary*

19

The Sporting Man's Tour of Europe
Wimbledon, Henley, Pamplona, and the Tour de France

Backpacking through Europe is a quintessential rite of passage for many an American college student. A buddy and I had our turn in 1991 when we waltzed on a shoestring budget through Madrid, St. Tropez, Paris, Munich, Budapest, Rome, and Barcelona packing in as many castles, cathedrals, museums, plazas, and bars as we possibly could in a span of fifteen days. We weren't ever quite sure where we would end up next. And that was half the fun.

Ten years later I returned to Europe for a more focused adventure—a themed adventure. Not around the proverbial Castles & Cathedrals, but around classic sporting events. By traveling in early July, I could add four notches to my *life experience belt* while completing a "Sporting Man's Tour of Europe."

Wimbledon

First stop, London. I hadn't scored tickets to Wimbledon in advance, but that didn't stop me from catching the train out to the stadium on the day of the semifinals and purchasing a grounds pass to soak in the ambience: purples, greens, and whites, and the immaculately manicured grounds. After thirty minutes of roaming the property, I felt smarter and more refined, as if by osmosis.

Of course I wanted a Centre Court view of local hero Tim Henman playing Goran Ivanisevic. Who wouldn't? But the real festivities took place on The Lawn, the slope of grass one hundred fifty yards behind Center Court where a large-screen TV flanked one end and vendors selling Pimm's and strawberries and cream lined the other. In the middle were five thousand partisan fans who had dubbed this space "Henman Hill." Some sat, some stood, some lay down, but everyone merrily followed the match while bantering with their neighbors, unafraid of being hushed by an umpire—more like "Opera in Central Park" than "Opera at Lincoln Center." Because of the proximity to Centre Court, I could still hear the grunts of the players and the gasps of the stadium crowd over the buzz of the Lawn social. Rain, however, spoiled the party (Ivanisevic finally defeated the local boy in five sets over three days), the volume died down, and I exited the grounds en route to my next adventure.

Henley

If Wimbledon scored an eight for refinement, the Henley Royal Regatta along the Thames the following day merited a ten. Well, at least in the morning. A buddy and I hopped the forty-five-minute train from Paddington Station to the medieval town of Henley-on-Thames, the perfect setting for a Hans Christian Andersen fable. The feathered hats and full-length gowns of the ladies hearkened back to the Royal Ascot horse races, while the brash purple, orange, and other eye-jolting blazers on the men seemed like 1970s game-show-hosts-gone-wild. Overall, it was a feast for the eyes along the pristine banks of the river, dotted with private white tents—the Henley equivalent of stadium corporate boxes—hosting late morning cocktails. As luck would have it, we stumbled into friends at a Yale tent—our golden ticket. For the next three hours, we sipped Bloody Marys and Pimm's and served as riverbank coxswains, politely cheering on boats from Cambridge, Oxford, and a smattering of Ivies that rowed by every ten minutes.

But by mid-afternoon propriety had disappeared, as if Bluto and his Delta fraternity brothers had crashed the party. Cups and bottles were everywhere; inebriated, disheveled bodies staggered to and from the trough bathrooms while others simply used the nearest tree or bush; and the occasional Victorian kiss and holding of hands had been replaced by wanton public groping. The refinement score had plummeted unceremoniously to a three. Perfect preparation, nonetheless, for my next stop where adrenaline would trump reason…

Pamplona

The third stop on *The Sporting Man's Tour*, following a trip through the Chunnel and an overnight train across the Pyrenees, was Pamplona, Spain, which for eight days in July hosts the Festival of San Fermín and the Running of the Bulls, transforming this relatively sleepy Basque town into the Mecca of global thrill-seekers, thanks in part to Hemingway's classic *The Sun Also Rises*. It's worth noting that in this rare case the English title is more poetic than the Spanish, but the Spanish title and Hemingway's original choice—*Fiesta!*—cuts more to the chase. I'd arranged to experience this *fiesta* with my sister and her friend who were travelling in Europe at the time.

San Fermín attracted two main types of runners: First, there was a small group of veteran Spaniards, largely Basque locals—the San Fermines—who had run with the bulls for years. They treated the race as a sacred event, the bull as a sacred animal, and meticulously prepared like die-hard New York marathoners. Then there was everyone else, a hodgepodge of Spaniards, of course, but predominantly an international crew. These folks caroused all night and by seven the next morning had barely slept a wink, relied on a shoot-from-the-hip game plan, and were unfit to run more than two hundred yards without bull-induced adrenaline. It resembled what might happen if the New York Jets invited eleven "lucky" fans at halftime to suit up for the second half against the Pats. And that's just it. You can bet that eleven fans—though maybe not the first eleven picked—would be willing to take a beating to brag about lining up against those "bulls." And you can guarantee that spectators would pack the stadium delighted to see such a slaughter.

Hoping to avoid slaughter myself, I approached the event more like the veteran Spaniards. I arrived well-rested, boasted solid aerobic and anaerobic fitness, and dedicated the entire first day in Pamplona to observing one running, asking questions, and developing my strategy. The most important lesson I learned was that if you fall down when the bulls are anywhere nearby, stay down. Repeat, stay down! Cover your head. Do NOT try to get back up until all the bulls have passed. Sure, you'll likely get trampled and bruised…*but you won't die.*

With the Golden Rule of San Fermín imprinted, the critical question became where to start. The course itself was just over a half–mile long and slightly uphill. It began at the stables on one side, turned ninety degrees to the left through a central plaza, and then turned ninety degrees back to the right before the finish in the bullfighting arena. Some suggested I run the first hundred meters, near where the locals chanted and sang just prior to the start of the race. But after watching this stretch the first day I realized two things: First, even though the bulls actually began their run on an incline, they charged their fastest on that part of the course, long before they tired. Runners here literally took three to five steps then dove to the side, somehow managing to dodge lightning. I wanted my run to last a touch longer than three heartbeats. Second, once the last bull entered the arena, the gate closed, denying runners still on the course the glory of rushing like a gladiator into the packed stadium and hearing the roar of the crowd. Since the bulls would likely take just two and a half minutes to run the entire course, only an Olympic eight-hundred-meter runner might be able to keep pace to the finish. Best to start further up. Of course, if you started too far up, you might enter the bull arena too quickly and never even see a bull…

My date with the bulls commenced at ten minutes before eight the next morning. I positioned myself in the plaza, smack in the middle of the course, and smack in the middle of hundreds of other red-and-white-clad, *Where's Waldo?* look-alikes. Everyone chatted away their nervous energy and waited for the barricade to lift at seven fifty-nine, allowing us to spread out along Calle Estafeta, the narrow straightaway walled in on both sides like a bobsled chute. About three hundred fifty meters from the stadium, I perched on a curb just eight inches deep, pressed against the steel-curtained storefront to gain a slight vantage point over the sea of runners. Eight o'clock. *Hisssssss. Boom!* We heard the rocket shot signaling that six bulls and six steers had just been released. They were coming straight for us.

What followed was one of the strangest feelings imaginable, perhaps like waiting for a twister to pass over your house, only you realized that you had deliberately placed your house in its path. Compounding the drama, onlookers two, three, and four-stories above peered down from their tiny, flowerpot-lined, black iron balconies, sadistically awaiting disaster like hockey fans salivating over a possible fight.

Eight o'clock and thirty seconds. Dozens of *San Fermines* walked by briskly, looking back over their shoulders every few steps. Soon the eerie silence was replaced by anxious murmurs and the shuffling of feet. Eight o'clock and forty seconds. *San Fermines* were now jogging by us *en masse*. The noise level grew as runners began to shout. We looked back toward the turn at Calle Mercaderes, now a sea of bobbing heads. Eight o'clock and fifty seconds. The river of bodies gushing by us peaked. We hadn't even spotted a bull, but our hearts were exploding. Then…we saw them. Two massive bulls shot by directly in front of us, and with adrenaline pumping at full-throttle, we jumped into the flow of madness and…RAN!!!

But where were *the other* bulls? The course was flooded with runners so the only way you could determine where the bulls were—at least before it was too late—was by reading the runners behind you: the greater the panic on the face and the more erratic the stride, the closer a bull. As I twisted around for a good look, another bull—all I saw were sharp horns—charged by a meter away. And that's when I charged, too.

I sprinted toward the stadium, navigated the treacherously tight entryway into the arena—a frequent human-bovine bottleneck—and threw my arms up in triumph. Although other runners now played a chaotic version of *matador* with the bulls scampering loose inside the ring, I didn't want to mess around, so I quickly hurled myself over the inner wall, content to spectate safely from the stands. Another American runner—apparently a cattle roper—actually wrestled one of the steers to the ground. But bad move—and a major viola-tion of the unspoken rule of "respecting" the bull. Immedi-ately a half-dozen Spaniards pulled him aside and kicked the shit out of him.

In a country known more for paella and sangria than numerical analysis, the local newspapers the next day pro-vided an impressive statistical breakdown of the run. My fa-vorite part tallied the number of injuries on each section of the course, broken down further by injury type, including contusions, fractures, and gorings. To humanize these stats, the adjacent page featured interviews with injured runners, now deified for their feat or folly, depending on your point of view.

The only thing that troubled me about San Fermín was that any joker off the street can participate. By contrast, in a marathon few people will enter unless they have invested the time—weeks, if not months—to prepare. In the Running of the Bulls, no barriers to entry means bleary-eyed revel-ers from the night before are running to your left, to your right, behind you, and in front of you. Your greatest dan-ger is not the bulls—it's the yo-yos who, with one awkward push, could send you stumbling into the charging herd, man or beast. It was totally unnerving. But hell, you still gotta do it. At least once!

The Tour de France

What better way to conclude my "Sporting Man's Tour of Eu-rope" than by catching *THE Tour*? Many cite the twenty-one-stage, two-thousand-mile-plus Tour de France as the most grueling competition in all of sports. Eager to catch a glimpse, we zipped from Pamplona by train to Grenoble, France, another picturesque city at the base of the Alps that became our hub for the week. This location allowed us to catch two stages of the Tour—the awe-inspiring L'Alpe d'Huez climb, a two-hundred-nine-kilometer leg featuring twenty-one switchbacks up nearly four thousand feet over the final fourteen kilometers; and the thirty-two-kilometer individual Time Trial from Grenoble to Chamrousse. The big news that year was, of course, Lance Armstrong. After nearly dying from testicular cancer, Armstrong had made a remarkable comeback and won the Tour in 1999 and 2000. But could he three-peat?

The Tour de France is one of the strangest events to watch in person. First you try to secure a prized vantage point along the course, then you wait. And wait. And then you wait some more. After four hours of waiting, a ten-minute caravan of support vehicles steamrolls through, followed by a ten-minute parade of tacky sponsor vehicles. Finally, in the *did-I-get-my-money's-worth?* span of three minutes, the lead rider breezes by, the last rider struggles through, and the rest of the colorful peloton including the yellow jersey blur everything in between. Then you call it a day and head home. It feels like going to Yankee Stadium to catch a game whose first eight innings are played at Shea, studying the scoreboard above an empty field, then watching the teams and cheerleaders storm the field to play the ninth inning live.

Not that you don't have a great time those first eight innings. We settled down on the spectacular French countryside *bleachers*—a thirty-degree grassy embankment a half-mile below the finish line at the L'Alp d'Huez ski resort. For four hours, we nibbled on baguettes, brie, tomatoes, and chocolate, all washed down with a couple of burgundies. We chatted with our Pan-European neighbors—tens of thousands of Spanish, Dutch, French, Italian, and other fans now lining the road—and we soaked up the summer sun and sweeping views of the valley below.*

Throughout our *picnic a la Tour* we received frequent updates from fans with portable radios. In one case, as the lead riders approached the base of L'Alp d'Huez, a German fan turned around and reported—in that same robotic monotone with which they might announce they are taking over your country—"Thee Ah-med-ican, yah, eez fay-ding. Yah." Our hopes were momentarily dashed. (We later learned that Armstrong had intentionally slowed to get some final words from his coach.)

But when the grade steepened, Armstrong took off after the leader, Jan Ulrich, and gave us one of the most thrilling moments in sport: the building, bubbling commentary on nearby radios in Italian, Spanish, and German; our periodic sighting of the dueling riders hundreds of feet below as they ascended switchback after switchback; and the flag-waving throngs bouncing alongside the road eager to sprint up the mountain in front of, next to, or behind the fast-approaching cyclists.

---

* The only downside was the ridiculously oversubscribed porta-potties—the nastiest I've ever seen. By the end of the day, the enormous mound of human waste protruded above the toilet seat like some dark alpine alien trying to escape. I opted to wait.

By the time the riders reached us, Armstrong had overtaken Ulrich and opened up a five-meter lead. He cruised to the finish line to win the stage and capture the Yellow jersey. The rest is history—he blew away the field in the Time Trial the next day and would not relinquish the jersey again in the Tour. Once again he would be crowned the champion, eventually riding to seven consecutive Tour victories. It was the perfect ending to a perfect "Sporting Man's Tour of Europe."

 Bonus Adventures: www.MyTop40at40.com
- *See Sporting Man's Tour slideshow*
- *Watch footage from the Running of the Bulls*
- *See Ironman New Zealand vs. Pamplona comparison*
- *Hear Kari's commentary*

20

My 9/11 Diary
Making sense of the Taliban

At eight forty-six in the morning when the first plane struck, I was en route to Uris Hall at Columbia University, bleary-eyed after a night of preparing cases for week two of business school. A couple dozen students stood in the lobby, their eyes glued to the handful of monitors showing smoke emanating from one of the Twin Towers. I didn't think anything of it. *Some bozo*, I figured, *doing some stupid stunt in a prop plane.* I charged up to the third floor, where our Creating Effective Organizations class was about to begin. An unusual flurry of whispers quickly spread the news that the crash had involved a major commercial airline, not a rinky-dink Cessna. Our professor asked us to focus on the matter at hand—a case involving Southwest Airlines. But just a few minutes later at three minutes past nine, a classmate opened the door to the classroom and announced with a pallid face, "*Another* plane just crashed into the *other* tower!"

At that point, a number of us shot downstairs where the lobby was now wall-to-wall with students fixated on the monitors. And then…the unthinkable: the South Tower collapsed. *What the fuck is going on?* Thirty minutes later, the North Tower collapsed. This was totally surreal. The only other time I'd felt even remotely close to that—where my sense of up and down was scrambled—was my freshman year in high school when I learned that the space shuttle Challenger had exploded. *That's just not supposed to happen.*

Within minutes, three classmates and I decided we had to do *something* to help, though we didn't have the foggiest clue what. One was a Brit who'd worked for Royal Dutch Shell, the other two were Navy officers fresh off duty from nuclear submarines. Although we barely knew each other, we started walking downtown toward the World Trade Center six miles away. Public transportation in the City was already frozen—within four hours all air space over America would be closed for the first time in history—but we could still use our feet. Surely extra hands could contribute something.

We started south from Columbia's campus at 116th and Amsterdam, speculating as we walked on what was going on, mixing in bits of our own backgrounds, and trying to comprehend the strange scene unfolding. As we skirted Central Park, two F-16s flew over us, performing barrel rolls as they zipped across the sky. We continued through Times Square, the world's capital of bells and whistles, where, for the first time, you could hear a pin drop. The streets were nearly vacant and the sidewalks almost empty, except for a silent stream of confused souls, like ourselves, walking, not quite sure where or for what.

We soon passed St. Vincent's Hospital near Fourteenth Street, the closest hospital to the disaster, where a traffic jam of ambulances created a cacophony of sirens and horns, the opposite of the eerie silence of Times Square. Then we walked another dozen blocks to Houston Street, where the police had barricaded the streets and would allow us no further. Beyond the barriers another mile down, we could see flames and smoke plumes shooting up into the sky, and all around us ash was lightly snowing down. There was nothing we could do. We took a long look, stunned, then simply turned around and started the six miles back, desperate to burn off adrenaline, desperate to make sense of it all…

Just two weeks earlier, everything had made *perfect* sense when I'd moved into my apartment in International House, a large residence between 122nd and 124th Streets on Riverside Drive on the Upper West Side of Manhattan. The nearly three hundred residents from around the world—primarily grad students at Columbia, NYU, the Manhattan School of Music, and other higher ed institutions—seemed a remarkably diverse group in a city already renowned for its mix of people. And on my first night in New York City when I joined some I-House residents for Turkish food, the Big Apple lived up to its billing.

I spent nearly the entire evening chatting with the trip organizer, a young woman from Tajikistan who spoke five languages fluently and was currently studying at SIPA, Columbia's School for International Policy and Affairs. I had barely heard of Tajikistan, but I had at least identified it as one of the former Soviet Republics in Central Asia. She described her upbringing in Afghanistan, not Tajikistan, where it turned out her father had been appointed by Brezhnev to "run the Afghan Province." She then recounted how in 1988 she and her family were evacuated in tanks as the Soviets pulled out of Afghanistan. I'd heard plenty of amazing stories, but this was the first *tank* evacuation…

Enthralled, I peppered her with questions. It turned out her family had then emigrated to France, and she ended up attending the University of Mississippi. Now, nothing against the University of Mississippi (after all, I'm from Oregon, which has taken its fair-share of tree-hugger, redneck, and hippy jokes), but after hearing her life story and how articulately she presented herself, Harvard or Yale seemed a more plausible choice. So I asked, "Why Mississippi?"

Her answer surprised me.

"My parents wanted me to keep a low profile," she responded. "There was this group called *the Taliban*…and my parents were concerned for my safety as a result of our connection to Afghanistan, so I could only go to the States if I agreed to attend a school that was *a bit off the map.*"

Ole Miss in Oxford, Mississippi would certainly qualify, but apparently even that wasn't enough. During her sophomore year she discovered that her parents had hired two secret service agents to keep an eye on her.

By now, this intriguing conversation seemed a perfect plot for a John le Carre thriller. Prior to this dinner, I'd never even heard of the Taliban—it hadn't yet entered the average American's lexicon. But just two weeks later, for all the wrong reasons, "The Taliban" was everywhere.

 Bonus Adventures: www.MyTop40at40.com

- *See front page of* The New York Times, *September 12, 2001*
- *Visit www.i-house-nyc.org*
- *Hear Kari's commentary*

21

Cuba Like It's 1953
A magical and nearly tragic night in Havana

Traveling to Cuba is like traveling back in time. At least when I visited in March of 2002, Havana looked like a war-torn city frozen in 1953, six years before Castro, Che, and the rest of their gang assumed power. Tons of prime real estate, including the Malecón waterfront and numerous colonial plazas, lay either vacant or in complete disrepair. Classic American automobiles from the early fifties—Fords, Buicks, Chevys, DeSotos, and Studebakers—filled the streets. Against a backdrop of sun-bleached pastels was a charming symphony of maracas, marimbas and the clink-clank of motors begging to be serviced.

It was also a place where a maitre-d, instead of simply telling us how to get to the nearest salsa hot spot, actually abandoned his post to escort us the six blocks to the club in the hopes of getting a two dollar tip—twenty percent of his

110

monthly wages (we gave it to him). It was a place where a line for ice cream—the national brand Coppelia—wrapped around the block (we sailed through the "Express Line" for tourists). And it was a place where prostitution was front and center, even leading to a casual conversation with the proud pimp of a well-known boxer (we learned he liked twins).

Like it or not, all that will likely change in the next decade once Fidel and Raúl pass the torch to the next generation. Havana could then turn into Varadero, the largest resort in the Caribbean eighty miles to the east, already a bland playground of pasty-white Canadians, Germans, and Italians looking for sun and sex. Or even worse, Havana may fill up with low-denominator franchise Americana: KFCs, Subways, and Mickey Ds. Cuba is like Berlin in eighty-eight—time sensitive. If you have a chance to see it, go now.

So when I heard that our business school was organizing a "study tour" of Cuba for Spring Break—a convenient way around the travel embargo—I signed up immediately. At the initial informational meeting, a friend leaned over to me and murmured with a dreamy smile, "Cuba…white dinner jacket, man!" Visions of Sinatra, Sammie Davis Jr., and the rest of those high-flying entertainers danced in our heads. Why not have a little fun? Brilliant—and I sprang into action.

Action, though, is often limited by funds. I could have shopped for a white tuxedo jacket at Brooks Brothers in midtown, but my student budget wouldn't go far in the silky retail world of Manhattan. Instead, after searching online and finding a low-cost outfitter in Tennessee, I found myself speaking with Skeeter whose banjo twang and name suggested he likely sold moonshine on the side. But Skeeter totally delivered. In just two weeks, my Rat Pack attire arrived. Two other buddies followed suit. When the time came, we'd be ready to set Havana on fire.

For a country that seems worlds apart, Cuba is mind-bogglingly close. Flying there was even anti-climactic. I originally envisioned a ten-hour flight, scrambling through tunnels, scaling fortress walls, then reciting secret passwords to Castro's sentinels to gain entry. Instead, the humdrum Continental Airlines flight was a direct fifteen-minute hop from Miami to Havana, the shortest of my life. Moreover, I learned that three airports offered direct commercial fights to Cuba—Miami, JFK, even San Francisco—for travelers on academic, governmental, and family visas. Suddenly it didn't seem so exotic anymore…

But our ten days were fantastic. We toured the tobacco farms in Pinar del Río and sampled freshly rolled cigars. We visited the sleepy Bay of Pigs Museum and the charming colonial seaside town of Trinidad. We explored Hemingway's beautiful villa and gardens, and we knocked back mojitos at his watering hole of choice, *La Bodeguita de en Medio*. As if that wasn't enough, we had tea with the American Principal Officer, the highest ranking U.S. diplomat in Cuba, and we enjoyed a wonderful home-cooked meal with the family of a classmate who had graduated from the top science high school in the country, attended university in the USSR, then sought political asylum in Canada with the dissolution of the Soviet bloc (only two of his fifty high school classmates, Cuba's best and brightest, still lived in Cuba). But it was our first Saturday night out in Havana—the *Night of the White Dinner Jackets*—that stole the show.

I had discovered that it was possible to hire one of the classy old cars, driver included, for somewhere around fifty US dollars a day. So Saturday afternoon I walked over to the Parque Central near the Hotel Inglaterra, where a number of "taxis" sat idle, and arranged for the driver of one particular gem—a 1953 emerald green Chevy Bel-Air with tinted windows and tail fins—to pick us up that evening.

At precisely seven o'clock, as our other classmates waited in the lobby to board our bus for dinner at the swank Hotel Nacional, we strolled down the main staircase sporting our white dinner jackets. All eyes turned. Two minutes later and right on cue, Antonio, our chauffer-for-hire, pulled up in his emerald beauty.

"Caballeros!" he called, then assisted us into the vehicle while our group looked on in disbelief.

What followed was one of those moments—like scoring the winning goal, landing your first kiss, receiving a standing ovation—that you play over and over again the rest of your life: Cruisin' in our classy car along the Malecón at dusk, overlooking the Caribbean, puffing on our Cohibas to the Los Van Van salsa soundtrack of horns, maracas, and cowbells. Magical. Not a worry in the world.

We intentionally meandered to revel in the moment and ensure that the bus arrived first so that when we finally drove up the stately, Royal Palm-lined, U-shaped driveway of the Hotel Nacional, we had the full attention of our own built-in paparazzi. Even Antonio preened while the flashes of our classmates fired away. You couldn't write a better script...

Or maybe you could. Fast-forward three hours. After poolside cocktails, a savory dinner, and an extravagant cabaret show, six of us decided to stroll back along the Malecón, puffing away on our Cohibas in the balmy tropical breeze. Despite a few safety warnings, we felt invincible, the heroes of our own journey. We swaggered along the poorly lit walkway—our incandescent cigar tips casting nearly as much light as the dirty street lamps, most of which didn't even work. The crashing surf below occasionally interrupted our conversation, which at that moment had turned to *The Godfather*.

I was flapping away about the shenanigans of the mob when suddenly, as if scripted, I disappeared. I hadn't noticed that a large concrete slab of sidewalk directly in front of me had caved in leaving a hole nearly three feet in diameter. My right foot plunged directly into the void, and everything from there on proceeded in slow motion.

As I free-fell forward, somehow I managed to rotate counter-clockwise one hundred eighty degrees, keeping my left heel hugging the edge and catching my elbows on both sides of the hole. My shoulder blades rested on the back edge. We could barely see anything and, as panic filled the air, I yelled, "I'm ok! I'm ok." At that point, one of my buddies shouted, "Kari, give me your hand!!" I tried to make sense of everything and simply repeated, "No, I'm… ok. I've…got it." At which point my buddy, whose baritone voice was as commanding as his stature, roared back, "KARI! GIVE ME YOUR HAND!!" I finally complied and he hoisted me to safety.

We could just make out the gaping crater in the middle of the sidewalk and gingerly crouched to see where it bottomed out. Nothing but blackness. I then held my camera directly over the hole and snapped a photo with a flash, revealing jagged rocks fifteen feet down where the surf splashed. A fall would have been ugly. By the next afternoon, members of our posse had already converted this spot along the Malecón into a side excursion for other classmates to show them the pit "where Kari almost died."

Remarkably, my white dinner jacket survived the episode unscathed: no rips, no scuffs, no stains. I guess I have Skeeter to thank. But best of all—and do not try this at home—I *never* let go of my cigar.

 BONUS ADVENTURES: www.MyTop40at40.com

- *See Cuba trip slideshow*
- *Hear Kari's commentary*

22

The Definition(s) of Good Service

Two views on dining out

Artur and Angela are fifty-something married executives living in the upper-middle class neighborhood of Botafogo in Rio de Janeiro, Brazil. They have been my private English conversation students for the past six months. We often chat about their extensive world travels, including many trips to the United States. Tonight, as we sit on their couch enjoying yet another *cafezinho*, I ask them what they like least about the States. They glance quickly at each other, roll their eyes, then blurt out in unison, "Eating out!"

For a happy-go-lucky couple who frequently weaves references to *moqueca na abobra*, *pasta fiorentina*, and other culinary delights into their conversation, it's a strange response, and I wonder what they mean. I anticipate the proverbial

116

attack on fast-food, a scapegoat everyone loves to hate (yet secretly loves), but their tag team explanation surprises me.

Angela: "Well, when we go to a restaurant in the States, not a minute after someone leads us to our table, a waiter appears with a menu and then comes back immediately to ask us what we want to eat." I can feel Angela's pulse rising.

Artur: "And no sooner have we ordered than the food arrives. We've barely exchanged a word of conversation when someone else interrupts us to make sure we're ok!" His hands are now flailing in the air as if he's fending off an army of attacking waiters. Then he hands the baton back to Angela.

Angela: "Next thing you know, we're offered dessert, but we've hardly taken a bite when they slap the bill on the table—and then they're shooing us away!" I'm stressed out just listening to them.

Four years later, I've just arrived in Havana, Cuba for a study trip where I join a dozen Columbia Business School students who arrived forty-eight hours earlier. One in particular, a prospective I-banker, fills me in on what I've missed as we ramble down a cobblestone street in Old Havana. With the extraordinary energy and efficiency of someone who has set a ten-million-dollar personal wealth goal before considering "what he really wants to do," he meticulously rattles off the group's itinerary to date. He then confides in me that the service in each Havana restaurant has been "absolutely terrible," uttered with the same disgust you might show if you were suddenly kissed by a troll.

"You're not going to believe it!" he begins. "We walk into the restaurant, sit down, and it takes *forever* for the waiter to bring us our freakin' menus. Then it takes *forever* for him to come back to take our order. I mean, I practically have to tackle the guy!"

His hands are now flailing, too, in what is clearly a painful re-enactment of his desperate efforts to flag down waiters.

"Jesus," he fumes, "the food *fiiinallllllly* comes…but *forget* dessert! *No way* are we tacking another hour onto this marathon meal." He's shaking his head in disbelief.

"And the check?!?! We almost walked out *without fucking paying*! We were there *forever*!"

I listen patiently and smile.

"That's certainly *different*," I comment.

"But that's not *good* service!" he declares, banging down an imaginary gavel.

 Bonus Adventures: www.MyTop40at40.com
- *Hear Kari's commentary*

PART FOUR
Age 31-35

23

Tongue-Tied
Face-to-face with Ricardo Montalban

The French have a great expression: *L'esprit de l'escalier*, or "The wit of the staircase." It refers to those awkward moments when you are tongue-tied and can't think of a proper response, only to have "that perfect line" come to you hours later while on a staircase, in your car, or anywhere for that matter when it no longer makes a difference. I once had exactly the opposite happen: precisely because the *perfect* line was already at the tip of my tongue, I was speechless.

I was living in Manhattan Beach and working at The Broad Foundation in Westwood for my business school summer internship, but when I arrived in California, I needed to take care of a pulled hamstring that I'd suffered from a soccer match the previous week. So I went to a doctor at a nearby UCLA clinic, and he prescribed four sessions of physical therapy over the next two weeks.

Given UCLA's fabled athletic history and impressive infrastructure, I imagined myself in PT sessions alongside world-class runners, Heisman candidates, and a host of NCAA champions from various sports. To my dismay, I discovered in my first session that I was three decades younger than the next closest patient—in other words, this was Geriatric Central. Not that it mattered. It just meant that the battery of circus tricks my physical therapist assigned me contrasted sharply from the activities of everyone around me.

On my fourth and final visit, I arrived on my lunch break, performed the usual drills with increasing speeds, weights, and motions, then returned to my "station" to change back into work clothes. Each station was simply an athletic trainer's bed with four "walls" of sliding curtains, similar to a hospital recovery unit. As I began dressing, I overheard what by now were familiar conversations. Through the left curtain: "Nice work, Mrs. Walker! Keep trying to lift your hand above your head." Front curtain: "Mr. Thompson, the swelling should subside in a couple days and you'll be back with your walker in no time." Right curtain: "Will I need to take these pills in addition to my heart medication?"

Then, I heard it. From somewhere to the right, beyond the immediate station, a rich baritone cut immediately through all other conversations: "EEN MY CONE-TREE, FREE-DOME EES NOTE A RRRRIGHT...BUT A RRREEESPONE-SIBEE-LEE-TEE!"

Who IS this guy? I chuckled to myself, buttoning up my shirt.

"JAMES," continued the *Rico Suave* monologue, "PLEES COME OVERR HERE...MY HEARING EES NOTE WHAT EET ONCE HWAS."

An older gentleman evidently of Latin American descent was conversing with someone a lot younger. My curiosity was piqued and I found myself eavesdropping, though the thunderous voice gave me no alternative.

"DAY-MO-CRACY EES AN I-DEEL, AN AH-SPEE-RAY-SHONE..."

As the political discourse continued, I couldn't help but think this was the most interesting conversation I'd heard in a while, certainly the most interesting in the therapy center. Generally given to sharing direct praise when warranted, I mulled over what I might say to this individual when I exited. As I pulled up my socks I thought, *I'll tell him exactly that—that this was one of the most interesting conversations I've heard for some time.*

But as I put on my left shoe I made a revision, *No, I'll tell him what folks often tell me: 'You've got a great voice. Did you ever consider doing voice-overs?'*

Then, putting on my right shoe I made my final edit, adding a touch of wit and humor, *I've got it!* I smiled smugly. *I'll say, 'Did anyone ever tell you that you sound just like Ricardo Montalban?'*

Beaming with confidence and primed to deliver the perfect line, I slid open the station curtain and strode toward the exit. At the end of the hall stood a diminutive, silver-haired gentleman in hospital workout clothes with a twenty-something young man seated next to him. I rehearsed my line once more, walked toward my target, then couldn't believe what I saw: not only did the older gentleman *sound* like Ricardo Montalban, he *looked* exactly like him, too!

I stared at him, he stared at me, and I was so thrown by the coincidence that my mind went blank. Totally blank. I didn't say anything, didn't even smile. I must have looked like a deer in headlights and he must have assumed that I was just another star struck fan. I turned my head away quickly and darted out the door, then froze in the lobby for a minute trying to make sense of what had just happened. When one of the doctors walked out behind me, I asked, "Um, excuse me…was…uh…that…uh…Ricardo Montalban?"

The doctor smiled and without missing a beat responded, "Yes. Yes it was."

 Bonus Adventures: www.MyTop40at40.com
- *Read about Ricardo Montalban*
- *Hear Kari's commentary*

24

Pimpin' in the Presidential Suite
A behind-the-scenes and under-the-sheets hotel tour

I've been to Detroit just once and distinctly remember how it challenged my sense of geography—after all, how can you possibly travel *south* across the Detroit River into Canada? It's gotta be *north*, until you examine a map and discover that the US-Canada border includes a strange aberration right around Detroit and Windsor, Ontario. Go figure. But the other thing I remember vividly is how I nearly got the bellhop fired just fifteen minutes after checking into my hotel.

I was staying at the Detroit Marriott, the highest hotel in North America and the seventy-three-story centerpiece of the GM Renaissance Center whose iconic black cylindrical towers anchor Detroit's waterfront skyline and represent the center of the automotive industry in the United States. My motive was work—as part of my business school summer internship at The Broad Foundation, we were piloting a program for urban school district superintendents and our first weekend training took place in Motor City.

I had just arrived on the Thursday night red-eye from Los Angeles, bleary-eyed and eager to get to my room. I followed the bellboy into one of the dazzling, central atrium elevators, where he pushed the button for the sixty-fifth floor—still to this day the highest floor on which I've ever slept. But I noticed that the elevator buttons extended up to the seventieth floor, a five-floor gap that piqued my curiosity and even provoked a tad of hotel-floor envy.

"So…what's on the seventieth floor?" I asked casually.

"Oh," murmured the bellboy who spoke with a heavy Hispanic accent, "That…is the Presidential Suite."

Now *that* sounded interesting, particularly since the dramatic pause in his delivery signaled that this floor was clearly off limits. I desperately needed a shower, a change of clothes, and a nap, but my first meeting wasn't until lunch and we stood alone in the elevator. Even at this early hour I thought, *If you don't ask, you don't get,* so I pressed: "Can I see it?"

Up to this point, the bellboy had fixed his gaze upwards just above the doors, the universal "safe-zone" for elevator passengers' eyes. He squinted and slowly turned toward me trying to process this request, as if I'd just asked to meet the Chupacabras. Finally realizing I was serious, he responded, "I'll, um, have to check with my boss…and see if I can get the key."

Perfect. We skipped the sixty-fifth floor and detoured to an administrative floor below, where I waited in the elevator while the bellboy obtained permission. Sure enough, he returned a couple of minutes later dangling a set of keys, and like a teenager picking up his first prom date, he awkwardly suppressed a smile, suggesting that he was even more excited than I was about exploring the private floor.

He inserted one of the keys next to the seventieth floor button, it lit up, and we were whisked to the top. And there it was, the Presidential Suite, a series of connecting rooms around the perimeter of the cylindrical tower. A circular hallway ran just inside, and across the middle were the elevators. I ditched my two travel bags and we began our impromptu tour.

After fumbling through his keys, the bellboy opened the first door while explaining that all the presidential entourages, including most recently those of Presidents G.W. Bush and Clinton, had camped out on this floor when they were in Detroit. A moment later, we entered the luxurious suite—more like a well-appointed home than a hotel—and I marveled at the floor-to-ceiling windows with panoramic views of the city and river below. I then turned and began walking toward the bellboy anticipating the next view, but he was walking back from what appeared to be one of the bedrooms and gently blocked my path.

"We, um, can't really, uh, go…in there," he stammered, somewhat embarrassed. His comment seemed strange, but I attributed it to his broken English as he led me instead in the opposite direction: "We can probably go through *this* door to another part of the suite…"

For the next three minutes, we worked our way through door after door as if completing a maze, each room leading to another room. Some spaces were geared toward eating or sleeping, others were designed for socializing or working, but every room boasted the same sweeping views. Before I knew it, we had walked the entire perimeter of the building, a complete circumnavigation of the Presidential Suite, and we found ourselves back in the elevator lobby near my bags, exactly one door shy of our starting point. Since the original door remained ajar, the bellboy walked over and closed it. *Another fine adventure*, I thought, glad to have had the experience of touring the exclusive seventieth floor.

But not ten seconds later, before we could summon the elevator, a fifty-something Frenchman in a white bathrobe stormed out the door into the hall.

"ZEES ees PWEEPOSTWEES!!! What ah you DOING een our WOOM? I can NOTE BELIEVE zees!" he fumed. "I weel HAFF you FIRED!" he shouted, his face beet red. I stood ten yards away next to the elevator trying to make sense of this odd encounter.

I quickly conjectured that when we had entered the first part of the suite, the bellboy must have encountered—*or exposed*—this high-altitude Casanova in the bedroom with his guest, prompting the bellboy's sudden change of direction. But why he didn't halt our tour, I have no clue. And why someone in the office hadn't mentioned an occupied suite, I don't know either, although I suspect an executive or client had simply scored the space as an off-the-books perk.

I do know, however, that once I was in my own room on the sixty-fifth floor, I began to feel guilty—*dude, I just got the bellboy canned*—and that pulled me right back down to the reception, where a huddle of bellboys was abuzz with gossip. I approached one of the supervisors to explain the situation and my part in it.

"No problem, sir, everything has been cleared up," she reassured me.

Then with a clean conscience, I returned directly to my room and took a much-needed nap.

 Bonus Adventures: www.MyTop40at40.com
- *Visit www.gmrencen.com*
- *Hear Kari's commentary*

25

Dramatic Arrivals and Departures

A business school adventure in Mozambique

Most air travel drama occurs during take-offs and landings—a perfect analogy of my trip to Chimoio, Mozambique, where I traveled in January of 2003 as part of a team project for a business school course on Private Equity in Emerging Markets. Our assignment? Develop a financing plan for the country's first rose farm. Our arrival and departure? Anything but a bed of roses.

The Arrival

Why travel halfway around the globe and not throw in some fun as well? A week before reporting for duty in Mozambique, my classmate from Argentina and I flew to Johannesburg to explore South Africa where we rented the ultimate safari vehicle: a shower-and-stove-equipped Toyota Hilux 4x4 with two rooftop tents on a roof rack and ladders dropping to the ground. If I'd had this rig growing up, I would have been the coolest kid at school. We toured Kruger National Park, cruised through Swaziland down to Durban, and then meandered up the balmy coast of the Indian Ocean on our own *Endless Summer* adventure. On our final day, we planned to cross over into Mozambique in the late afternoon, join our two other team members in the capital city of Maputo for dinner, and catch the morning flight up to Chimoio after a good night's sleep.

But then we learned the bad news: the border station on the southern edge of Mozambique near Ponta d'Ouro, for whatever reason—baboons, a taxi strike, trade embargo, flood waters, or any of those random reasons that keep life interesting in places like Mozambique—no longer issued visas. Now, the only way to obtain a visa was to backtrack south, cut inland, cross Swaziland again including both immigration checkpoints, and enter Mozambique via Lebombo on its western border: a detour of roughly three hundred miles. We had just four hours to make the nine o'clock office closing time in a vehicle designed more for surviving elephant stampedes than for setting land-speed records.

Swaziland Round II—a great name for a video game—was a green blur of bananas, sugarcane, and other crops on the periphery while we bore down on the road and focused on the speedometer and clock. *7:15? 8:03? 8:36?* Remarkably, we crossed the Mozambican border at Lebombo minutes before the office closed and secured our visas. Now we just had get to Maputo, one hundred kilometers southeast. In the dark.

Night driving in Mozambique was rumored to be even worse than night driving in Baja California. Crater-sized potholes, animal corpses, tree branches—an array of obstacles could wreak havoc when you least expected it. It didn't help that Mozambique, due to its civil war a decade earlier, was second only to Cambodia in undetonated landmines.

Then there were the police. The night before at our campsite, a South African traveler had given us an odd piece of advice about Mozambique: take a cooler stocked with cold beer. Not for the heat, as we imagined, but to pay off the police. A liquid bribe. Mozambican cops were notorious for pulling over foreign vehicles, finding "violations" that warranted a fine, then agreeing to resolve the dispute immediately for a smaller *payment*. This guy had simply invited the police to help themselves to a couple of brewskies each time he was pulled over as if the cops were long-time friends, thus lubricating his way through the country. With our three-hundred-mile helter-skelter detour, we'd forgotten this crucial currency, our own cooler of beer.

Within five minutes, we were flagged down along the dark highway at a police checkpoint. The lone officer brandished an automatic weapon. "Papers, please," he requested in Portuguese. It was clear from both his breath as well as his gaze that Mozambican firewater flowed through his veins. He mumbled something, returned our papers, and to our relief let us on our way. But this didn't bode well. *Drunk. Cop. Machine-gun. Darkness.* Those four words make for a nasty combination.

Two stressful hours later we rolled into the capital city, where our hopes of quickly locating the hotel vanished: Few streets were labeled—and even fewer were illuminated. We felt like blindfolded shoppers fumbling our way through a ramshackle mall and inevitably drove in circles. Then, the police lights flashed. *Shit,* we swallowed hard, *here we go again.*

An officer in uniform emerged from the darkness on the right side of the vehicle—the driver's side on South African vehicles—and ordered me to roll down the window. He, too, clutched an automatic weapon, and he, too, slurred his speech like someone only a drink away from getting cut off at the bar. We had just travelled the wrong way on a one-way street, he explained, as if the pitch-black corridors even deserved to be called streets. He confiscated our passports—*would he return them?*—and disappeared back into the night, though we overheard him arguing with two colleagues about what to do with us. I immediately shifted all but the equivalent of five US dollars into my sock.

Minutes later the officer returned. Evidently we'd need to appear in court to pay our fine…it was quite complicated…*muito complicado*…could take weeks…unfortunate, really. Long pause—my cue: "Boy, we're *really* in a hurry. Isn't there *some way* we could pay the fine right now?" I inquired, kicking myself for forgetting our beer cooler, but simultaneously revealing the small stash of bills in my wallet. His glassy eyes now focused and he handed back our passports, glanced over both shoulders the way drug dealers do in movies, then instructed me to place the "fine" money into one of the passports. I complied and he carefully opened the document with one hand while pocketing the money with the other, returned the passport a final time, then bid us goodbye and drove off.

But we were still lost. Hopelessly lost. And it was now 1:00 a.m., and we feared more unsettling interactions with drunk, corrupt police and wondered if we'd ever find the hotel. In desperation, I did the equivalent of firing a flare: I drove to the US Embassy, the only recognizable building several hundred yards back, parked near the anti-car bomb cement bastions running the perimeter of the building, approached the lone soldier on duty at the illuminated guard post, and explained the situation. Two walkie-talkie calls later, three uniformed military officers exited the main building, politely introduced themselves, boarded a nearby vehicle, then escorted us through the dark labyrinth of Maputo to our four-room hotel. After my buddy and I let out a huge sigh of relief, he confessed his amazement: "The Argentinean Embassy would have told me to piss off!" *God Bless the USA*.

We didn't sleep well that night, but at least the next morning we caught our flight to Chimoio after one final challenge: Filling the gas tank of the rental vehicle. Thanks to the humongous tank, high price of petrol, and significantly devalued Mozambican currency, I withdrew one million Mozambican *meticais* (a few hundred dollars), then promptly blew my fortune on a tank of gas.

The Departure

We'd just spent an incredible two weeks in the outskirts of Chimoio learning the ins and outs of a rose farm. We'd heard the amazing story of the white Zimbabwean owner who had started the rose farm, a man born and raised in Zimbabwe (formerly Rhodesia), who spoke several tribal languages fluently, and even had represented his country in the Tokyo Summer Olympics for field hockey. Yet just one year earlier as a result of the changes under way with Mugabe he'd been forced at gunpoint to leave the land he'd farmed his entire life. He had held off the marauders for four days before finally fleeing over the Mozambican border with his family. Now he was living in a tent. But that's another story...

When our project concluded, we boarded the small *Linhas Aéreas de Moçambique* plane at the Chimoio airport and looked forward to a peaceful afternoon in Maputo some two hours later. At least that was the plan. Instead, we were unexpectedly rerouted to Beira, thirty minutes to the east, where we were told we'd need to change planes. In Beira, we waited on the tarmac a few hours for our next plane—a tiny Russian six-seater, including the two seats for the pilots. The interior resembled an old-school van from the eighties, more lounge than plane, with four seats spread out in a square atop a shag carpet and no physical separation between passengers and cockpit.

We finally took off. Barely. The plane groaned like a hippo might sound if it suddenly took flight. The din and vibration of the engine were horrific. After ten minutes, with our nose still pointing upwards at a thirty-degree angle, it became clear we weren't climbing anymore. The captain began shouting at us over his shoulder—either the plane had no intercom or that just wasn't his style: "Our landing gear hasn't retracted, and it's creating a huge drag."

"But no problem," he assured us, smiling. We simply maintained our angle and elevation, about five hundred feet above the ground, all the way to Maputo, as if we'd opted for a leisurely afternoon of aerial sightseeing. Three and a half hours later, we landed in the capital, glad not to be a random statistic. We dined late that night on sumptuous tiger prawns, sipped cold beer, and early the next morning, eagerly hopped a plane out of the country on our way back home.

 Bonus Adventures: www.MyTop40at40.com

- *See South Africa and Mozambique slideshow*
- *Hear Kari's commentary*

26

My Date with the IRS
Surviving an audit

Naughty—that's how I felt when the one-page form letter from the Internal Revenue Service arrived. The letter began innocuously enough: "We have selected your federal income tax return for the year shown above for examination," as if I were the lucky winner who'd soon be choosing between a new car and a Caribbean vacation. But Uncle Sam and his friends at the Treasury were really screaming, "Cheater!" After thirty-two years of striving to keep a clean record in life, I suddenly felt as if a scarlet dollar sign had been branded on my forehead: I was being audited.

The next day my embarrassment turned to anger. *Morons!* I thought. *If anything, the government probably owes me money. What a waste of time!* For more than ten years, I'd spent hours and hours trying to comprehend the various forms and prepare my tax statement correctly. Just recently, as a full-time graduate student, I had earned a ten-week salary from my summer internship so paltry it even qualified me for an additional stipend from my university, and this was my only income source. When I double-checked my work, I discovered I'd indeed made a mistake: it seemed the Treasury owed *me* six hundred dollars. I licked my chops and imagined a team of IRS officials on their knees begging for forgiveness. I couldn't wait for my appointment.

The thirty-story IRS building in midtown Manhattan is the polar opposite of Disneyworld: no rides, no castles, and no one wants to see Mickey. Outside the drab gates, a queue of nearly one hundred zombies—all in dark suits with gloomy faces—snaked along the sidewalk. After thirty minutes in the security line, I rode the escalator to the main lobby where I was given a number and directed to a waiting room…and waited some more along with fifty others. Every few minutes a smiling IRS official appeared—kind of like the guy at the zoo who feeds mice to the snakes—called out a number, then escorted the person into a nearby elevator. No one ever saw the mice return.

After thirty more minutes, I, too, joined the snake-feeder in the elevator. He seemed pleasant enough, but I kept quiet. When the elevator doors opened on the twenty-fifth floor, we stepped out into a sea of filing cabinets so deep I nearly lost my balance. We walked down the hallway, and still all I could see were grey filing cabinets. We turned a corner… another sea of filing cabinets. *Was this some sort of sick interrogation tactic?* We proceeded to a door at the end of the hallway, which I took to be the IRS agent's office, so I started mentally rehearsing my case as he nudged open the door. But instead of a desk, family photo, and a plant, I saw twenty people sitting around the perimeter of an otherwise empty fifteen-by-fifteen foot room, still waiting—mice about to be dropped into the snake cage. In fact, these were the same twenty mice who had preceded me below. There was one empty chair.

"Please wait right here," the agent instructed before closing the door and leaving.

After another thirty minutes, I finally met with a legitimate IRS agent—*the Examiner*—whom I'd envisioned would resemble Agent Smith in *The Matrix*. Instead, the Examiner's name was Michael. He said hello, shook my hand, thanked me for coming in, then quickly cut to the chase: I'd claimed two types of education credits on my tax return when I was entitled to only one. We reviewed my return together, the way a third grade teacher might walk through a recent math quiz with a pupil, and the calculation in question went something like this:

a) *Multiply your age by three*

b) *Subtract your total years of education*

c) *Multiply this figure by the interest rate on your largest student loan*

d) *Add half of last year's tuition*

e) *Divide this by seven*

f) *If the number is even, you get credit A. If the number is odd, you get credit B. But if the number is prime, you get both!*

He was right—I'd screwed up. There'd be no apology from the IRS, and no refund check. Instead, I owed the government one thousand dollars. I handed over a check, signed the proper forms, thanked the agent, and was escorted back down the elevator. I left the building with three thoughts:

These guys are good.

I'll never prepare my own taxes again.

We should simplify the tax code!

 BONUS ADVENTURES: www.MyTop40at40.com

• *Hear Kari's commentary*

27

A Giant Named Radomir
A prodigious mentor for an Andean peak

We all need mentors to succeed in life. *Amárrate a los buenos y serás uno de ellos. Stick with the great ones— and you'll become one, too.* Parents, teachers, coaches, relatives, colleagues, and others can all fit the bill. So why not track down your own guide?

That's exactly what I did in September of 2003 shortly after joining the staff at The Dwight School in New York City. My goal at the time was to climb Acongagua, the highest mountain in the Andes just shy of twenty-three thousand feet and the highest peak outside the Himalayas. But my training grounds—New York City, barely above sea level and flatter than pita bread—were far from optimal. While on my own I could piece together cardio workouts, stair climbs, and frequent travel to mountains, I needed something more…I needed a coach. I decided to roll the dice and seek the guidance of legendary, yet controversial, faculty member Radomir Kovaevic, an Olympic medalist in Judo and modern-day samurai whose novel approaches to athletic development had been profiled in *Sports Illustrated*.

Towering over everyone at six feet five inches and two hundred eighty pounds, Radomir barely fit through the School's narrow hallways. He taught physical education as well as philosophy, but his official title was "Master Teacher." Though raised in Bosnia and Serbia, Radomir attended university in Japan and became the first non-Japanese to win their National Judo Championship. He later competed in three Olympics, winning a bronze medal in the Moscow Games. Along the way, he had mastered five languages and become passionate about helping others, particularly children, develop a warrior spirit to extract the most out of life. He'd witnessed his own country plagued by corruption and violence and wanted to escape. On a trip to the States, he gave an emotional address about freedom to the students at Dwight, and *on the spot* was offered a work visa by the Head of School as well as a platform for his ideas.

Not that everyone was receptive to his ideas. While younger children gravitated toward him like lion cubs to their father, older kids—particularly teenagers in the middle of the academic and athletic spectrum—generally gave him wide berth. But there were two exceptions: First, elite athletes wanting to compete on an international level and willing to be masochistic in their training. This included ranked fencers, tennis stars, basketball players, sailors, and even figure skaters. Radomir could mold a champion. Second, Radomir worked with the down-and-outs, the students that drove teachers mad, the incorrigibles who because of either family issues or medical conditions like Tourette's had simply been written off. Radomir knew how to turn them around.

Having identified my perfect guide, I visited Radomir one afternoon in his office where he smiled and gestured for me to sit down. His office was a cave of news clippings that he'd pasted to the walls over the years—photos, stories, and headlines showing violence, elation, and the just-plain-weird. At first glance, it seemed a little Hannibal Lectorish, like the strange cutouts of a serial killer that might allow the prime-time detectives to zero in on their suspect. But look again and you would detect one simple theme—the extreme of the human condition. Here was an athletic Freud, a life-long student of motivation, someone who loved dissecting the emotions that drive us all, and an alchemist who combined these ingredients in just the right sequences and amounts to produce…Greatness.

He looked calmly into my eyes as I explained my proposition: Would he like to add "mountaineer" to his list of disciples?

"Yes," he answered firmly. "I have some ideas. I will think about it some more."

He invited me to his "Radomir's Workout" later that week when we'd begin our training. I thanked him for his time and he responded with a slight bow of his head: "Thank *you*, sir!"

Joining a Radomir Workout was akin to dancing in the ballet, performing in the circus, and serving as a lab rat all at the same time, only with a Darwinian sense of competition driving your every move. Classical music blared across the "stage"—a Spartan room with fifteen stations of logs, Russian kettle balls, and other strange contraptions that looked as likely to be used for evil as for conditioning. At center stage stood Radomir, the lab scientist testing what was possible, the Grandmaster choreographing the rotation of bodies from point to point and exhorting everyone—in both uncensored Serbo-Croatian and English—to push faster, higher, stronger.

Goni se u picku materinu! (Literally, Go back to your mother's pussy!) Do you know what that means? Go back to where you came from! From millions of sperm, WE are the ones who made it. We are ALL born winners! We are ALL born champions. But you must continue to FIGHT and prove that YOU deserve to be here.

The next four months of workouts would be a constant battle with my own limits—just when I thought I had mastered one challenge, Radomir would invent a variation to raise the bar. But on that first day, my *very first* workout, as we were wrapping up and I was thinking to myself, *This wasn't such a big deal,* Radomir called us into a circle.

"Good work, my children!" Radomir bellowed, punctuating his words with yet another exclamation point. "Now *this* man here…" Suddenly Radomir was pointing at me. "He is going to climb a very…big…mountain so I have *one more* exercise for him." Twenty-four teenage eyeballs were now fixed on me.

Radomir grabbed one of the twelve-foot balance beams that rested just a few inches off the floor and propped up the far end on some large blocks so that it was now three and a half feet off the ground, with no mats anywhere in sight. Then he instructed a lanky senior who weighed a buck-fifty to jump into my arms. I braced myself for the heavy load, placing my arms out in front of me, and the student latched onto me like an odd honeymoon bride.

"NOW," commanded Radomir. "CARRY HIM to the TOP of the balance beam!!"

I nearly shit my pants. *This guy's crazy*, I thought. But of course I already knew this. This was the man who had dangled briefcases of cash—tens of thousands of dollars—in front of parents to challenge them on what their child's life was worth. This was the same guy who had hammered nails through the soles of shoes to cure flat feet. And this was that very same "Master Teacher" who, when a teen pounding a sledgehammer into a truck tire had been distracted and smashed himself in the face, sent the bleeding boy to the emergency room alone to teach him responsibility, only to provoke a near-lawsuit from the parent, yet win eternal loyalty from the student. *Was I now headed to the ER, too?* One wrong move and I'd easily break a leg, or worse. And if you think I was scared, that was nothing compared to the poor student in my arms who would have been thrilled to go home and complete that calculus assignment he'd put off.

I took a couple of unsteady steps forward, set one trembling foot on the balance beam, pushed off with my other foot, but had no equilibrium and landed back on the ground. With the precious human cargo still in my arms, I tried once more. One foot up, OOOPH! Then the other, UHHHH! We were on the beam. With no view of my feet and my legs and arms trembling, I swung my right foot in front of my left. A step! Then quickly, my left foot in front of my right. Another step! I'd travelled one-fourth the distance and was about eighteen inches off the ground, still far from the forty-two-inch summit. I took a deep breath, lunged forward again, but this time lost it. We both tumbled to the floor, bruised, but not beaten.

In those three minutes, Radomir had hammered home to all of us a key lesson of the Vince Lombardis, the Jose Mourinhos, the Phil Jacksons, the Chris Carmichaels, and other sculptors of athletic dynasties: you must train in practice and in everyday life with the same, if not greater, conviction and intensity as in competition. He was dead right. In my case, on a mountaintop in high altitudes where every step requires a herculean effort—and one misstep can be fatal—you need to have absolute confidence and concentration in every move. And you sure as hell better be in damn good shape. I learned my lesson in Workout One. Four months later and just days before my expedition, I successfully carried my partner up—and back down—the full length of the balance beam.

Tragically, Radomir was felled three years later by prostate cancer. Until then, no one had conceived of anything, including illness, that could even slow this invincible, larger-than-life figure. But one afternoon, just a few weeks before I left for the climb, I had discovered a tiny soft spot in his armor. We were three-quarters through the usual workout and I was exhausted. Frequently, Radomir would tug your shirt, slap you, push you backwards, or pull other tricks to impede your movement—just to toy with your mind and force you to give that extra effort while keeping your composure. But this time as I moved between stations while two prospective parents observed—Radomir routinely entertained visitors from all over—Radomir hoisted me into the air with a gigantic bear hug. I couldn't budge.

"Get to the next station! " he ordered. "C'MON! GET TO THE NEXT STATION!" I could wiggle my feet and my head, but that was it. He continued provoking me, "WHAT ARE YOU GOING TO DO? HA! HA! HA!"

His thunderous cackle and ferocious scowl were all the more intimidating since my head was just inches from his face. I was spent—and not even an extra burst of energy would overcome his gorilla embrace. And that's when I used the one thing I had left, the only remaining arrow in my quiver: I stretched my neck as far as I could, and planted a tender, wet smooch on his cheek. It was hard to shock Radomir, but *that* did it. He laughed—relaxing his monstrous hold—and I dropped. A nice reminder that sometimes the only thing more powerful than a sword…is a kiss.

End Note: When I returned from my successful climb, Radomir gave me a copy of Ivo Andric's Pulitzer Prize-winning novel, *The Bridge on the Drina*, with the following inscription: "Kari, Hardship has made a jewel of you." Vintage Radomir, a man as gentle, compassionate, and erudite as he was fierce and inspiring.

Bonus Adventures: www.MyTop40at40.com
- *Visit www.dwight.edu*
- *Read* Sports Illustrated *article*
- *Watch Kari's Aconcagua video including Radomir workout*
- *Hear Kari's commentary*

28

A Steamy Love Story
How I discover my princess...in Argentina

Everyone asks me how I met my wife, Ximena. And I like to tell them—because I couldn't have written a better script. The short answer? We met at the airport in Mendoza, Argentina. The long answer, however, is more interesting...

In December of 2003 I flew to Santiago, Chile en route to Argentina to climb Aconcagua. What's amazing about Argentina, like Brazil, is that the closer you get, the more beautiful women you see. Both countries are factories of beauty. So I wasn't surprised to spot half a dozen very attractive women on the connecting flight over the Andes into Argentina. One in particular—with almond eyes, cascading dark hair, provocative curves, and an air of spunkiness—*really* caught my eye.

When we landed in Mendoza, I brought up the rear of one of the two lines for immigration. The woman I'd been ogling stood last in the other line. I brainstormed ways to strike up a conversation, but ultimately kept my mouth shut and simply admired her out of the corner of my eye. She passed through immigration ahead of me, quickly retrieved her luggage, and left. Considering her a sample of what was to come, I thought to myself, "This is going to be a *great* vacation in Argentina!" *María. Alejandra. Victoria.* Many evenings, many possibilities…

Instead, for the next fourteen nights I squeezed into tiny tents with sweaty, hairy Slovenian-Italian dudes with names like Igor and Boris. The expedition was a blast—just no Marías or Victorias, not even close. Yet the day I returned to the Mendoza airport to fly back to Santiago, I discovered among the hundreds of random passengers the exact same girl I'd been checking out earlier. *What a wild coincidence.* Again I began thinking of ice-breakers to start a conversation, but I quickly gained perspective: If some random joker with a foreign accent approached you at an airport all Guy Smiley and declared, "I could swear I saw you two weeks ago here at the airport!" would you really engage in conversation? Once more, I remained silent.

Thirty minutes later, as luck would have it, she was sitting at my gate, waiting to board the same flight. A seat sat empty next to her. I immediately took it. At this point, I might have tossed out my hook except for one pet peeve: I detested Argentinean pretense. Just as I loved the down-to-earth beauty of Brazilian women, I hated, at the time, the haughty airs and unapproachability of Argentineans, typified by the Porteñas from Buenos Aires. So rather than feed egos, I did exactly the opposite: I stuffed my own face with two ice cream bars, avoided eye contact, and struck up a conversation *with someone else*—an American guy, evidently a mountaineer, a few seats away. Our conversation turned to Mendoza, where we recounted strolling through quaint plazas, wandering the eucalyptus-lined streets, and sipping malbecs while gazing at the Andes, which prompted my comment, "Mendoza is very beautiful." And that's when I heard a sweet voice to my side in near perfect English interrupt and correct me, "*ARGENTINA* is very beautiful!"

My long-awaited opportunity. I forgot about the fellow mountaineer and directed my attention to this beautiful *señorita* at my side.

"Ah, you speak English! Where are you headed?" I asked.

To Los Angeles, where she taught Spanish at a boarding school in nearby Claremont, California. I didn't tell her that I, too, worked in education, or that I'd lived six years in Los Angeles and even knew Claremont quite well.

"Did you move there from Argentina?" I continued.

No, she had taught for two years at Deerfield Academy in Massachusetts. I didn't reveal that I also knew that prep school reasonably well since a number of my Dartmouth classmates had been Deerfield grads.

"And how'd you end up at Deerfield?" I pressed.

She had completed her Master's in Education at the School for International Training in Brattleboro, Vermont. I didn't mention that I'd attended college an hour north of Brattleboro, or that two friends had studied at SIT, well-known in international education circles. In this three-minute *pas de deux*, I learned that she spoke English fluently, her background surprisingly paralleled mine, and despite my preconceptions about Argentinean women she was actually quite cool, which I defined, for better or worse, as someone who laughed or at least smiled at all my jokes. As we boarded, my head was spinning.

She settled into the plane's first row while I plodded all the way to the last row. We couldn't have been seated further apart, but this didn't faze me. During the flight, I scribbled down my personal email and cell phone on a business card, figuring I'd casually hand it to her once we arrived in Santiago where we'd resume our conversation. But in Santiago, I was literally the last guy off the plane aside from the pilots and stewardesses. Passengers in transit proceeded to the left, while those disembarking in Santiago— I was spending a week in Chile—immediately descended stairs to the right. As a result, I stood alone on the staircase scratching my head—*the beautiful señorita* was nowhere in sight. Somehow—blame my Quixote illusions—I actually thought she'd stick around to continue the conversation.

Here's where a healthy attitude helps. I allowed myself to brood for all of five seconds, then thought, *Hmmm, I know her first name is Ximena with an "X," and I know she has some Arabic last name. I also know where she works. I'll follow up when I get back to New York.*

Sure enough, a week later when I was back in New York City, I looked up The Webb School in Claremont. Their website contained a page describing the Foreign Language department which listed the teachers along with their email addresses. All but one included a photo—a teacher named Ximena

Allub. *The beautiful señorita.* What have I got to lose? So I sent her an email.

Now believe me, I thought long and hard about this email. There were a number of approaches I could have taken, but the email had to be innocuous lest I appear like a stalker. I ended up sending the following, the most important written composition of my life up to that moment:

Subject: Aeropuerto Mendoza
From: Kari Loya xxxxxxx@columbia.edu
Date: Sat, 10 Jan 2004 18:18:57
To: xallub@webb.org

Ximena:

Well, Aconcagua may have fried my nose and lips, but my memory remains intact, and I managed to remember your name and the name of your school from our brief conversation in the Mendoza airport. How on earth did someone from San Juan ever end up in Claremont?

Based on its website, Webb looks like a very cool school and an interesting place to work. OK, Claremont may not exactly be a cultural mecca, but right now with the temperature outside in Central Park at roughly the same as at Camp III on Aconcagua, I'll swap you two weeks of NYC culture for a couple weeks of warm California sunshine…

A couple questions:

1) *How DID you end up at Webb? I noticed several other faculty from SIT as well. Does SIT have some sort of exchange with Webb?*

2) *When are you organizing the next cool Spanish trip? (spring break??)*

3) *How do you like the 24/7 boarding school life? (!) A buddy of mine taught Spanish at St. Andrews in Delaware a few years back. Great experience, but tiring, and you never really get away.*

Ah, many questions, but I'll limit myself to these three…In the meantime, get your website photo/bio up to speed with the rest of your colleagues (!), then make sure you rent some skis/snowshoes and take the tram from Palm Springs to the top and journey up Mt. San Jacinto! (Afterwards you can read Borges, Cortazar, or Neruda in the Jacuzzi…)

Cheers,
Kari
(el gringo del aeropuerto)

And she responded. Immediately. Emails led to phone calls, phone calls became longer phone calls, and finally these calls prompted our first date and many coast-to-coast visits over an eighteen-month courtship (thank you, Jet Blue!). I'll spare the remaining details, but would like to highlight three things:

First, a week after we began chatting on the phone, I received a photo of her in the mail out of the blue. She looked just as I had remembered—beautiful. She, in turn, requested a photo of me. The only photos readily accessible were from my recent Aconcagua trip, and most showed my head hidden beneath goggles, balaclavas, and hats. I finally scrounged up one post-expedition shot of me smiling alongside five, fifty-something Italian-Slovenians while feasting at McDonalds (I had proposed this international exchange of culinary favorites: they treated me to gelato, then begrudgingly allowed me to treat them to McDonalds). I emailed her the photo and was shocked by her response: "*Which one are you?*" Ouch. I was more than fifteen years younger than everyone else in the photo. I suddenly felt like the dork who waves back to the pretty girl only to discover she was greeting her boyfriend behind him. Yet rather than deflate my spirits, her question lifted them—if she couldn't remember what I looked like, that meant she'd been drawn in by our *conversation*. I reasoned that was a good thing.

Second, on the evening of our first date, a Valentine's Day candlelit dinner at Le Colonial on West Fifty-Seventh Street, just as dessert was served and we recounted our first conversation in the Mendoza airport, I revealed that that was not the first time I had seen her. As you can imagine, her face momentarily blanched while thoughts of serial killers danced through her head. I quickly explained that I had been on a flight two weeks earlier and could have sworn that she'd flown on the same flight. She had. The brief tension vanished and we enjoyed the rest of the evening.

Finally, throughout our courtship, we faced the challenge of managing romantic expectations, from that heavily anticipated first date to every ensuing bi-coastal encounter. We ice-skated at Rockefeller Center, sipped poolside cocktails in Santa Monica, flirted our way through Universal Studios, and spent a weekend in Vermont among other adventures. But did sparks fly every moment we met? Not at all. Sure, we definitely enjoyed our time together, but if we'd expected sparks twenty-four-seven, we would have set ourselves up for disaster—and I wouldn't be writing this story today. This was more like Harry and Sally telescoped into a year—simmer patiently, then bring to a boil. And above all, avoid *hyperdating*, that dangerous trap high-achieving professionals can easily fall into where every time they get together they do amazing things, but they never do the *real* things that happen in *real* relationships. Reality is Wednesday morning when you're both tired, cranky, and late for work, yet someone still has to do the dishes. We washed plenty of dishes together.

Our relationship blossomed as I had hoped, and precisely a year to the day and hour that I laid eyes on her for the first time, on a Sunday morning when she least expected it, while we were both in Argentina again, I proposed. Ah, *amore*! Now with such an elaborate courtship, one would expect an equally elaborate wedding. Details found in the next chapter...

 Bonus Adventures: www.MyTop40at40.com

- *See Kari's first photo of Ximena*
- *Hear Ximena's side of the story*
- *Hear Kari's commentary*

29

Anatomy of a 007 Wedding
Bridezilla and Groomzilla's
three-day James Bond wedding

O ur wonderful courtship could have been a movie script. How could we top that? By making our three-day James Bond theme wedding in Argentina unforgettable. Here's how we did it:

1. **Exotic locale.** Hong Kong? St. Tropez? Marrakesh? In our case, we opted for San Juan, Argentina, part of the sunny wine region at the foot of the Andes Mountains, which also happened to be my wife's hometown. Bond would be right at home eating the world's finest steaks and sipping the world's greatest malbecs.

2. **Hollywood invite.** Our two-minute risqué movie trailer—the only wedding invitation of its kind that I'm aware of—included a mini-poster with press fanfare. The first

part established that I was 007, but had decided to retire thanks to my newfound romance, throwing M into a fit; the second announced an elite competition in Argentina involving secret agents from around the globe (friends who submitted action photos) to select my replacement. The contest was dubbed "The Search for the Next 007." And the overall movie's title? "This Tango Lasts *Forever.*"

3. **Profile the players.** Every one of our eighty international guests was assigned a secret agent number (from 001 up to 080) and given a *debriefing* packet when they checked in at the hotel. Included was a "Search for the Next 007" t-shirt with their numbers on the back, a schedule of events, and most importantly, a list of all the "secret agents" with a few witty notes about each guest that captured why we admired them. This profiling served two main purposes: first, it served as yet another wonderful ice-breaker. *Ah, 013! Aren't you the one that…*And second, it was a creative way to share meaningful words about friends and family.

4. **Friendly competition.** A contest can get the juices flowing. During the two days prior to the wedding, our guests took part in four distinct competitions: wine-tasting, polo, an adventure race, and tango as a way for everyone to get to know each other and experience some of the "Best of Argentina."

5. **Consideration for everyone.** Any good teacher *differentiates* instruction…

a. **Wine-tasting.** This was straightforward. Everyone toured a local winery and participated in a preliminary tasting before trying to identify the varietal of five mystery red wines. Nothing like wine to warm up the crowd.

b. **Polo.** This event was a bit trickier. We all watched a chucker (one period) of a match, and afterwards those who were interested could snap a souvenir photo astride a stationary horse while donning full polo gear including hat, boots, and mallet. But the elite group with solid riding experience—six of our esteemed guests—completed several drills to test their equestrian ability and skill with a mallet while a jury made up of other guests awarded points for best performance.

c. **Adventure Race.** Here everyone was divided into three groups. The first took an easy hike around the base of the dry and craggy Tres Marías hills while the second took a stiff hike to the top. The third started several miles away and completed a spectacular loop, scrambling up boulders on one side, running across the razor-thin ridge, and descending the same path as the other hikers before crossing the finish. Everyone who competed in the polo competition and adventure race first signed a legal waiver. *A wedding with waivers.* Bond *really* would have been proud.

d. **Tango.** Who doesn't smile at the possibility of dancing a tango? Everyone participated in one of three tango classes the first day and learned the same sequence of steps to "El Choclo." The instructors then selected our finalists—the top two male and female dancers in each group. The following evening at our awards dinner—the night before our wedding—professional dancers and a live tango quartet entertained the crowd. At the end of this performance, we invited the finalists from the classes onto the floor to strut their stuff to "El Choclo" and impress a jury of peers.

6. **Costumes!** Everyone loves the chance to break out of stiff wedding attire. At the awards dinner, guests dressed up to a Bond/Tango/Hollywood theme: a sexy, swashbuckling Honey Ryder (*Dr. No*); a lacy, seductive Countess Lisl Von Schlaf (*For Your Eyes Only*); a head-to-toe gilded Jill Masterton (*Goldfinger*); and an eclectic bunch of villains all showed up.

7. **Prizes.** You can't have a competition without prizes! Our winners received a medal on a blue and white band mirroring the colors of the Argentinean flag, and the medal itself bore an inscription: *Campeón de Vino, Campeón de Polo, Campeón de Aventura, Campeón de Tango.* We also threw in a *Campeón de Disfraces* for the most creative costume. The last medal was the *Campeón de Distancia* for the guest who had traveled the farthest—our winner had

journeyed over eight thousand miles, starting in the Arctic National Wildlife Refuge and hopping seven flights over three days to join us! (The runner-up had traveled over seven thousand miles from London.) And of course, we also gave a prize to the overall winner, *The Next 007*—a large Roger Moore doll purchased on eBay.

8. **Surprise.** A fifteen-minute "Steamy Love Story" video screened at the awards dinner not only playfully recounted how we met, but also revealed a secret that only our immediate families knew—that we'd actually been married by "Elvis" in Vegas six months earlier. Two-thirds of the way through the video, the narrator (me) proclaims, "And there was only *one place* capable of consecrating such a fairy-tale romance." The camera then cuts to real footage of Elvis marrying us in The Hollywood Wedding Chapel. "Yes," I testified to address the growing murmurs, "We got married in Vegas!"

9. **Brazilian *carnaval.*** One minute Bond is in Monaco, the next he's in the Caribbean. We couldn't quite pull *that* off, but since an Argentinean wedding typically runs until seven in the morning, it's important to electrify the crowd at critical points to keep the energy strong. Two hours after the general dancing started, scantily-clad Brazilian samba dancers strutted their way into the winery to a jolting *batucada* percussion. Gyrating hips. Hot pepper feet. Flying feathers. A new wave of energy hit the revelers, helped along by two-

hundred-plus custom-made, colorful Nerf hats. Nothing like a playful prop to help folks cut loose and lift a party to greater heights.

10. **Soundtrack.** It wouldn't be a Hollywood production without capturing the music to relive the memories. Our party favor—aside from the foam hats and secret agent t-shirts—was a CD of the key songs our guests heard during the three-day celebration. The James Bond theme from the original trailer invite, the tango everyone danced to, a couple favorite disco tunes, and others. Cool Experiences + Accompanying Music = Future Smiles whenever you hear those tunes.

 BONUS ADVENTURES: www.MyTop40at40.com
- *See wedding poster invite*
- *Watch wedding trailer*
- *Watch "A Steamy Love Story" video*
- *See wedding slideshow*
- *Hear Kari's commentary*

30

Cannonball Run
Racing circuitously cross-country

When my fiancée suggested in 2005 that we hire a company to drive her vehicle the twenty-five hundred miles from Claremont, California to New York City as part of her move east, I balked—why would I pay *someone else* to have all the fun? Besides, a solo cross-country trip would be the perfect opportunity to check off three other goals: 1) Touch the bottom of the Grand Canyon, 2) Amble through the French Quarter of New Orleans, and 3) Knock off three of the six states I'd never visited— Arkansas, Louisiana, and Mississippi. The only hitch was that this itinerary stretched to four thousand miles—and my work schedule left me just five days to complete the journey. But my eyes lit up and pulse quickened. It would be a veritable Cannonball Run!

163

Stop #1: The Grand Canyon

Jogging down the dusty Bright Angel Trail at five thirty Sunday morning in desert solitude, with ruby, gold, and orange peeking over the towering Canyon walls and the stars still twinkling high above, feels like dancing with angels. Ponderosa and Pinyon Pine perfume. Baby white aster necklace and Indian paintbrush earrings. Warm, breezy kisses every few steps. As I danced downward through hundreds of millions of years of geological history, however, I couldn't shake two nagging thoughts directly related to the twinge in my neck and the rumble in my belly: First, *why didn't I splurge on the lodge instead of the no-frills torture slumber in the driver's seat of the car?* And second, *why did I eat that midnight prime rib?* I'd flown to Claremont late Friday night, started my drive Saturday afternoon, reached the National Park in complete darkness, then clearly abandoned all sensible "prerace" strategies for sleep and diet. And now I was blatantly disregarding the Grand Canyon National Park's information brochure which strongly discouraged hiking the five thousand feet down to the Colorado River and back in a single day, a twenty-two-mile challenge that carried the risks of exhaustion, dehydration, and sunstroke.

I coasted down the trail and regularly plundered my stock of Gatorade, peanut M&Ms, and other high-calorie goodies from the South Rim gift shop. Within just two hours, I crossed the Silver Suspension Bridge over the mighty Colorado and strolled into Phantom Ranch—a collection of stone and wood cabins—where overnight river runners and hikers were beginning to stir. I officially touched the bottom

164

of the Canyon by perching myself on a rock near a brook, then soaked up the desert sun for fifteen minutes while taking in the sights. A five-inch lizard scampered across the path before pausing for some amphibian push-ups. Two brilliant butterflies fluttered above a prickly pear cactus, then tested their wings in the soaring canyon walls above. Off in the distance, three bright yellow rafts floated peacefully downriver, a moment of tranquility before navigating the Class V monsters downstream. And all the while, I guzzled as many liquid calories as possible in preparation for the ascent out of the formidable canyon.

With the June sun now blazing, I crossed the Black Suspension Bridge then set off on the South Kaobab Trail to complete the spectacular loop. *Slow and steady, slurp, slurp, slow and steady, slurp, slurp* became my mantra as I negotiated countless switchbacks up the dry, red dirt. The sweeping views were jaw-dropping—including the three-hundred-sixty-degree view of the Canyon at Skeleton Point. At one turn, I passed a group of twenty or so mule-bound tourists plodding down into the Canyon. My heart throbbed, my lungs heaved, and my skin sizzled—but I didn't envy this group one bit. By eleven thirty, I was back at my car with a newfound appreciation for the magnificence of the Grand Canyon. I'd completed the twenty-two-mile adventure in six hours—and I felt like one of the legendary Tarahumara warriors of Mexico's Copper Canyon.

But the Cannonball Run clock was ticking. I changed clothes, hopped in the car, and stopped at a gas station for a celebratory forty-eight-ounce Mountain Dew, PepsiCo's gift to extreme athletics. I then drove five hundred fifty miles to a cheap hotel in eastern New Mexico and slept like a baby.

Stop #2: New Orleans

I had originally envisioned rolling into New Orleans Monday afternoon, taking a leisurely nap followed by high tea in the gilded lobby of the classic Fairmont Hotel (severely damaged two months later by Hurricane Katrina) where I'd booked a room. I'd savor the cuisine, music, and ambience of the festive French Quarter late into the evening—then reality hit: I'd somehow mentally leapfrogged a couple of states and still needed to drive thirteen hundred miles to get there.

So finally, at nearly three in the morning, just as sugar and caffeine had lost their resuscitation capacities, I pulled into New Orleans and checked into the hotel. No nap. No tea. No night on the town. Instead, I staggered to my room and collapsed on the bed for the second straight night.

But just because I'd blown the evening didn't mean I would squander the morning. I arose at seven and walked several blocks to the French Quarter with its two and three-story colonial buildings and admired their terraces, lamp-posts, flowerpots, and shutters that hearkened to a bygone era. Sleep deprivation added a wobble to my gait, but other early risers probably assumed I'd just stumbled out of the last watering hole. Walking through the French Quarter in the morning, though, is a bit like walking the stadium bleachers three hours after the game. I may not have experienced the *real* New Orleans, but hell, at least I'd made it inside the stadium.

I wandered over to Café du Monde on the corner of Jackson Square—the historic Place d'Armes—for some much-needed café au lait and beignets, the deep-fried fritters sprinkled in powdered sugar that should be renamed "Breakfast in Heaven." To my delight, a tuba, banjo, trombone, and clarinet fired up some Dixieland jazz, a nice accompaniment to the excellent early morning people watching. After a leisurely hour and a half, I crossed the street to my final New Orleans stop, the Corner Grocery, and ordered their famed muffuletta sandwich to go. Incidentally, beignets at Café du Monde and muffuletta at the Corner Grocery hadn't originally been on my itinerary, but they sprang up moments after completing the Grand Canyon run.

"Did you now just run that thang?" a sixty-something couple asked me incredulously as I emerged from the South Kaibab Trail. They were from New Orleans.

"I'm headed to New Orleans next!" I responded, keeping in mind the advice to *always wear your interests on your sleeves*, "Any suggestions?"

And just like that I'd discovered two gems.

Stop #3: Three Elusive States

Early Tuesday evening, I settled down at a barbecue joint in Jackson, Mississippi and devoured ridiculous amounts of beef and pork ribs, brisket, and everything else buried under the fingerlickin' good sauce. Washed down with a nice pint of ale, the meal seemed a fine way to celebrate having finally set foot in three elusive states: Arkansas—cruising the rural highways at twilight in the western part of Clinton Country en route to New Orleans; Louisiana—largely a caffeinated blur at night then a wonderful morning in New Orleans; and now Mississippi—greener than I ever imagined and home to some mighty tasty barbecue.

The clock, of course, was still ticking. One more cheap motel, lots of talk radio, and one truck stop later, I woke up at the crack of drawn for the final sprint into New York City, just ahead of rush hour traffic. I unloaded the car, showered, and arrived at work for my Thursday morning meeting at nine. Four thousand miles in five days. Solo. And only one minor, *strange* brush with the law...

It happened in eastern Oklahoma en route to Louisiana at sunset on one of those rolling country highways where the sixty-five miles per hour speed limit suddenly drops to thirty-five because you just entered some invisible town made up of a silo and a toolshed. The caffeine was flowing, music was blaring, and *hoo ha!* I was bound for New Orleans! Precisely when the blue and red flashing lights appeared in my rear view mirror.

I can only imagine what the officer was thinking—*Silver Mercedes SUV with California license plates? Ha! Sounds like some fffun...* I pulled over to the side of the road followed by the sleek white sedan and watched my side mirror nervously as the trooper approached.

"License and registration please," said the officer, whose tattooed biceps were bigger than my thighs. His massive fists—the kind that induce nightmares—sported two lavish, inscribed rings. *A former linebacker, perhaps, for a championship Sooner team?*

When I handed over my ID and the paperwork for the vehicle, he surprised me: "Why don't you come back and join me in the car while I check this out."

Now I've been pulled over a half-dozen times, but I've never had a cop invite me *into his car*. Was this simply friendly Oklahoma police protocol—or the dangerous first step toward becoming a Pulp Fiction gimp? Regardless, I wasn't in a position to argue.

I followed the officer back and sat in the passenger seat of his car while he called in my information to run a report. The vehicle seemed remarkably sporty for a police car: beige leather upholstery, no wall divider, and only ceremonial rear seats where a rifle hung across the back. As I responded to his questions with "Yes, sirs" and "No, sirs," I still couldn't tell if I was a kid on a cool field trip or about to be led to the Deliverance darkside.

When the dispatcher finally came through with a clean record, the officer explained he'd give me just a warning this time and handed back my ID. Awkward at best, but that was it. I thanked him, apologized for the mishap, and returned to my car. I never mentioned the Cannonball Run.

 Bonus Adventures: www.MyTop40at40.com
  - *See Grand Canyon run slideshow*
  - *Watch Grand Canyon video clip*
  - *Watch Pete McBride's short film "Chasing Water" about how the Colorado River runs dry*

31

Yemeni Tea
Dubai and the power of branding

When my wife and I planned a Spring Break vacation to Dubai in early 2006, I came across a remarkable statistic: one-quarter of the world's construction cranes were rumored to be in Dubai. As soon as we landed at the airport, our observations confirmed this stat. Cranes were everywhere. In Manhattan you might spot a billboard promoting the new Trump Tower or some other high-rise scheduled for completion in eighteen months. In Dubai, you'd see a billboard touting the new Media City—a collection of thirty such high-rises—scheduled to open in half the time. New York City seemed sleepy, even timid, by comparison.

We stayed the first six nights with my wife's friends in Deira, the historic part of the city, exploring the bizarre mix of old and new: dining outdoors at Damascus restaurant where waiters from Lebanon, Jordan, Syria, and Egypt served our meals with cardamom-infused pita bread, piping hot and puffed up like blowfish; wandering through the gold and spice souks where, besides jewels and spices, goods such as Iranian caviar and camel's milk reminded us of this unique trade route; shopping in elegant malls that rivaled anything in the States and included food courts where mothers in full burqas carried trays of McDonald's Happy Meals to their children. We even met with real estate brokers who regaled us with over-the-top projects like The World—a man-made collection of private islands just off the coast in the Persian Gulf which, viewed from above, resembled a map of the continents.*

For our last three nights, as part of a delayed honeymoon, we opted for more lavish quarters—the Royal Mirage Palace, arguably the nicest lodging in Dubai aside from the Burj Al-Arab, the self-proclaimed "Seven-star Hotel" whose vertical sailfish structure soared into the sky just down Jumeira beach. We looked forward to privacy, pampering, and comfort.

Immediately upon entering the spacious lobby, we sensed luxury—marble floors, tapestries, elaborate mosaics, and dramatic color combinations of ruby and gold—making it clear that this was no ordinary hotel. We had entered an Arabian oasis, the ideal spot to hear all one thousand one of Scheherazade's tales, perhaps over a good hookah. As we sat on a sofa waiting to check-in, a smartly uniformed attendant with a charming accent offered us a plate of dates and

---

* Except for the last page, the brochure looked like anything you might see out of Southern California or Florida—a family enjoying a barbecue, a little backyard croquet, and a dip in the pool. The last page, however, revealed a *Bengal tiger* frolicking in the surf—a plausible image in a region of the world that prizes exotic pets.

what she referred to as "Yemeni Tea." *Yemeni Tea.* The name alone conjured up images of flying carpets, magic lamps, and dusky princesses. We savored the ambience, nibbled on the dates, and sipped our tea in no hurry at all.

After several minutes of silence, my wife and I stared at each other with tea cups in hand and chimed in unison: Best. Tea. Ever. Softly sweet like a fairy tale, warm and spicy like a starry night, this was Arabian mystique in liquid-form, the sort of beverage served moments before entering Heaven. Surely Sheik Mohammed Al Maktoum himself drank this same elixir, *Royal Family Tea.*

When the attendant returned, I asked if she would share with us how they prepared Yemeni Tea and imagined ancient secret recipes, closely-guarded tea fields in Yemen, and exotic ingredients available only to a select few. Instead, she pulled back the curtain on the Wizard of Oz, glanced over both shoulders, smiled sheepishly, and then whispered, "It's Lipton Tea with cloves!"

 Bonus Adventures: www.MyTop40at40.com
- *See Dubai trip slideshow*
- *Hear Kari's commentary*

PART FIVE
Age 36-40

32

Reverse Therapy
Unloading my demons in a voice-over session

My favorite voice-over gig of all time was for the Xbox video game "True Crime: Streets of New York." When I arrived punctually at the west side studio for the job, I sported my usual attire—a suit and tie—much more formal than most other voice-over talents dressed for stage and on-camera work. The receptionist escorted me to a lounge and I settled into one of the chairs, enjoyed a drink, and waited. Ten minutes passed and no word from anyone. Another ten minutes. Still nothing. A gentleman appeared, looked around perplexed, and left without saying a word. Five minutes later, the receptionist wandered back to say that everyone was waiting for me. I walked down the hall and entered the studio where the same gentleman I'd just seen—evidently the producer—sat between three clients and across from the engineer.

"Ah, so *you're* Kari?" he greeted me. "*You* speak Spanish?"

My blond hair (what's left of it) and blue eyes routinely throw people.

"Claro que sí, hombre!" I fired back.

He laughed, then quickly confessed, "I thought you were his agent!"

He then handed me the script for the "M for mature"-rated game in which I would play three roles: a slimy street gangster, a corrupt museum curator, and a ruthless drug lord—all of Latin American origin. Nearly every line was dirty. I threatened, blackmailed, tortured, and sexually harassed a number of helpless souls in the raunchiest words I knew, a full sixty minutes unloading every filthy comment imaginable as well as unleashing an exotic array of grunts and other sounds. The noises alone exacted sweat:

Yell as if you're falling off a two-story building: "Ahhhhhh!"

Ok, now it's a thirty-story building: "Ahhhhhhhhhhhhhhhh-hhhhhhhhhhhh!"

You were just punched hard in the face: "Uff!"

Great, now you were punched in the stomach: "Urrr!"

Hit the guy back: "Hoo-wah!"

Now punch both attackers: "Ha! Hoo-wah! Ha!"

At the end of this intense session, I laughed—I'd never felt better. Shortly before, I'd stepped off a busy midtown Manhattan street into this place bearing my share of daily worries. I'd left my real life behind and entered the persona of characters as far from my normal self as anyone could imagine. Then, for an hour, with a green light to be bad, I'd pumped my vilest emotions and thoughts into the microphone, letting the profanity rip like a pent-up Catholic schoolboy with Tourette's finally having his catharsis. I got everything off my chest while five people listened. *And listened attentively.* When it was over, I felt amazing, light as a feather, honor roll-clean and completely purged. And to top it off, these "shrinks" were going to pay me! It was like therapy in reverse. I couldn't help but think the world would be a better place if everyone performed in video game voice-overs, specifically the "M for mature"-rated games, baring their souls, letting out their demons, and collecting a nice fat check.

 Bonus Adventures: www.MyTop40at40.com
- *Hear Kari's voice-over demos*
- *Hear Kari's commentary*

33

Vox Clamantis in 07202

The Wall Street Journal shows how far from the Joneses we've moved

M oving out of Manhattan feels likes committing so-cial suicide. So when my wife and I sought more space, but refused to pay the outrageously skyrocketing rents of early 2007, we thought long and hard before leaving the Upper West Side. Standard options for our peer set included Brooklyn, Westchester, even Queens, Hoboken, and Jersey City. But go any deeper and we'd fall entirely off the map. Our move to Elizabeth, New Jersey signaled not only our adamant refusal to *keep up with the Joneses*, it exclaimed we were *ditching* the Jones altogether.

We were drawn to Elizabeth by a close family friend and the relatively inexpensive real estate, but New Jersey's fourth largest city had other pluses as well. Like in Manhattan, we could still walk a block to get milk, a newspaper, or a prescription at the pharmacy—conveniences hard to forego after living in the Big Apple. We also enjoyed nearby Warinanco Park—less polished than Central Park (no Geese Police!) but largely free of camera-toting tourists and the strict regulations that often made Central Park more museum than park. Finally, we liked the mix of ethnicities around us: the Indians and Pakistanis who owned the gas stations and played cricket; the Portuguese who flew their red and green flags next to the Stars and Stripes outside their homes; the Orthodox Jews who were among the earliest residents in the area; and the pan-Latin crew that accounted for most of the music in the air and made parts of Elizabeth feel like San Salvador, Bogota, or Montevideo.

But Elizabeth was rough at the core. After all, this was Tony Soprano's stomping ground, and Mickey Rourke's down-and-out character in *The Wrestler* frequented the nearby Cheeque's strip club. That twinkling night skyline off the Jersey Turnpike? Merely lights on oil refinery towers and smokestacks. All of this inevitably corresponded with crude behaviors: residents who littered, even in their own driveways; pedestrians whose profanity exceeded "pleases" and "thank yous"; and my favorite—drivers who jumped green lights to make left turns, beating the oncoming traffic and giving a heart attack to anyone stepping into the crosswalk.

These negatives seemed to scream out anytime a middle or upper-class professional familiar with New Jersey asked me where I lived. Summit, Chatham, or Westfield—no problem—but Elizabeth? Eyebrows raised quizzically, then apologetically, as if I had just confessed to having a venereal disease. Next would come the awkward, but well-intentioned follow-up: "How did *you* end up in Elizabeth?"

Yet it was my subscription to *The Wall Street Journal*—my first ever and a way to take advantage of my new seventy-five-minute commute—that hammered home just how far from the Joneses we'd travelled. Three weeks into the service, the paper didn't arrive. At first, I suspected newspaper theft. *How dare they?* But after several days *sans Journal*, I dialed the company's delivery hotline to complain, and the next day the paper appeared.

Four weeks later, the same deal. When I called again to complain, the representative apologized mechanically in one of those highly-trained voices to keep the pit bulls at bay and awarded me a free month-subscription. Service resumed the following day. This frustrating pattern continued: *No paper. Complaint. Free month-subscription.* By month seven, the situation had become absurd. When I no longer bothered to complain, several weeks passed without a newspaper. I dreamed of strangling the delivery guy.

And that's when it dawned on me. I recalled my own days delivering the *Eugene-Register Guard* in high school where I earned the same amount of money—something like three cents—for each paper delivered. As a result, I dreaded the outliers requiring extra time. These customers lived in homes with long, sloping driveways and demanded that their paper be tucked under the doormat or at such-and-such an angle just inside the screen door, or worse still, they lived several blocks from the rest of my customers. I secretly wished they'd cancel their subscription. *Was I now the outlier?*

When I called the hotline that evening, my tone shifted from impatient to curious. After proceeding through the usual motions—*complaint-apology-free month-subscription*—

I posited my theory to the customer service representative, the same way a philosophy professor might begin a lecture to provoke discussion: "Your delivery guy is intentionally avoiding me because I'm too far off his normal route."

"No, sir," the rep responded, quickly dismissing my comment.

But I pressed: "Well, can you tell me then what other houses are on the route?" Now she was the one losing her patience.

"Sir, there are lots of houses on each route," she interjected. "I can't possibly break it down like that." But then she softened.

"What is your zip code again?" she asked.

"07202," I answered calmly. *CLICK-CLICK-CLICK-CLICK-CLICK* came the sounds of her keyboard, then a long pause.

"Well, that's strange…" she mused aloud, as if her terminal had just vanished. "Usually when I type in the zip code, a bunch of addresses appear on my screen…but yours…yours is the only one popping up!"

I laughed, not in a way that said, "See, I told you so!" but rather with the pride of a kid who possesses the shiniest, newest bicycle on the block. I was the lone voice crying out, *vox clamantis*, the lone *Wall Street Journal* subscriber in 07202. Nonetheless, I politely declined the additional free month and did not renew my subscription.

 Bonus Adventures: www.MyTop40at40.com
- *Hear Kari's commentary*

34

The One-Way Run Commute
A creative strategy for the daily grind

One of the biggest obstacles to happiness is a long commute. When my wife and I moved to New Jersey from the Upper West Side of Manhattan, turning my enviable seven-minute, door-to-door walk into a *seventy-five-minute, car-train-subway circus*, I quickly realized I was in deep trouble.

At best, I got home late in the dark, too wiped out to exercise. At worst, I got tied up on the subway, missing my train in Penn Station then improvising dinner with a couple slices of pizza while I waited for the next train alongside middle-aged commuters sporting various stages of pot bellies. It was a brutal first year. I gained ten pounds, softened at my core, and flagged in my overall energy. I was dying a slow, suburban death by commute.

Then it hit me: *the one-way run commute*, easily my best idea of the year. On Monday mornings I dress in business attire while toting a garment bag with suits, shirts, and ties for the week, plus a running outfit. At the end of the workday, I hang my suit in a closet, tuck my dress shoes away, stuff my Oxford and tie into my backpack, and then don running gear. With that, I'm off for a jog three miles straight down Eighth Avenue to Penn Station—from Eighty-Ninth Street where I work to Thirty-Fourth Street in midtown. I hop on the train to Jersey, ride for thirty-two minutes, and then run the final mile and a half home where a quick shower awaits. The next morning I do the car-train-subway shuffle back to work wearing clean running clothes, change into a suit and tie in my office, then repeat the cycle at the end of the day. Friday evenings I pack all my business clothes back into the garment bag and reverse the Monday morning trip with my wife picking me up at the station in New Jersey.

This new routine is brilliant. I fit in my workout, plain and simple. And I make it home just as quickly as before. In fact, I now miss far fewer trains and have far less downtime in Penn Station. No more peering up the subway tracks waiting for the B or C line that never seems to come. Instead, a quick glance at my watch tells me to quicken my pace if I'm running behind. Third, the endorphins and blood flow from the exercise perk me up so that I can read, write, or plan on the ride to Jersey and not simply slump into slumber. Lastly, I score serious points with my wife who shares the commute with me in the morning but returns two hours earlier so always drives the car back home first and now doesn't have to pick me up until Friday.

This run is not a Zen experience—no focus on one step at a time, controlled breathing, and mind wandering while entering a zone of peace with the world. It's more like being tossed into a washing machine with a load of New York City landmarks and icons, then battling to get out alive. Down Central Park West, the main obstacles are doormen darting out of their prized park-view buildings and dog walkers grasping nearly-invisible dog leashes.

Sweeping between Columbus Circle and Time Warner Center onto the bike lane on Eighth Avenue, Chinese delivery bikes kamikaze from all angles, yellow cab doors fly open, and Central Park carriage horses drop land mines en route to their stable. Outside the Worldwide Plaza at Fiftieth, I *OJ* through a fleet of black Lincoln Town Cars and Chevy Escalades waiting to shuttle away executives. While billboards and Broadway marquees fight for my attention, I focus on avoiding the Fed Ex handcarts, roving Sabrett's hot dog stands, and briefcase-toting pedestrians now engulfing Forty-Second Street.

At this point, I've nearly broken free. I leave behind Madame Tussaud's, the signs promoting "private gentlemen's shows" around Port Authority, and the steel-girded *New York Times* Building whose facade looks custom-made for the X-Games. I blow by Gray's Papaya whose perpetual two-dogs-and-a-drink "Recession Special" is remarkably decoupled from bull and bear markets. Finally, I salute the spire of the Empire State Building to the east as well as the cylindrical concrete vault known ironically as "The Garden" directly ahead, and I descend into Penn Station.

It's one thing to run in July—it's a totally different story in the dark, icy depths of February when I began this new routine. February is the reason people move to Florida. But good gear helps—I sport Gore-Tex tights, Solomon all-weather trail shoes, a SportHill long-sleeved stretch fleece top, Pearl-Izumi three-fingered AmFIB cycling gloves, an REI balaclava exposing just my eyes, and my Mountain Hardware fleece hat. Every article of clothing, though reflective, is predominantly black—a tell-tale sign that I've lived in New York for a while. For greater visibility, I strap on a blinding Petzl halogen headlamp. The end result? What might pass for standard commuter attire in the Pacific Northwest makes me look like a freak in Manhattan.

This became clear on Day Three of my new run commute. I was cruising down Central Park West in full winter running regalia when several blocks ahead, next to a dimly lit park bench I spotted a shopping cart piled eight feet high with plastic bags of aluminum cans, quite an engineering feat. Next to the cart stood a slightly hunched-over homeless man with a bushy, gray beard and a horseshoe ring of rust-colored locks cascading down from his bald crown. He wore tattered clothing and ranted away while flailing his arms in the air as if conducting an imaginary symphony. Still twenty yards away, I could hear him grumbling in gibberish as I approached. Had he been auditioning for a gnome in a new Pixar production, he would have nailed the part. And that's when he turned his head and spotted my headlamp, which in the darkness looked like a UFO.

"WHAT the ?%&$!?!!!??" he shouted, shooting both arms up toward the sky and staring at me with eyes like saucers. "LLLOOK at this NNNNNUTTJOB!! LLLOOK at this NNNNUTCASE!!!" He rotated counterclockwise as I jogged by giving him wide berth.

"LLLOOK at this LUUUUUNATIC!!!" he yelled, simultaneously turning and waving his arms until he'd done a complete three-sixty. I continued south and his ranting faded in the distance.

In a city of trailblazers, visionaries, and go-getters, it can be hard to leave your mark. But when the craziest of the City's homeless are calling me a "nutcase," I know I'm beginning to leave mine.

 Bonus Adventures: www.MyTop40at40.com
- *See One-Way Run Commute slideshow*
- *Hear Kari's commentary*

35

Just Do It

Rubbing elbows with a budding
author and a Hollywood star

Extraordinary generally flows from regular people taking a very large number of ordinary steps. These individuals simply put one foot in front of the other and keep at it to reach their goals, be it scaling Mt. Everest or pursuing any other grand ambition. From afar, it's easy to lose sight of the discrete parts and instead marvel in complete awe at the end point. But meeting these high-achievers face-to-face makes these *journeys-of-a-thousand-miles* seem remarkably doable—and gives me the confidence to take that critical first step.

When I struck up a conversation with the blond guy a few years younger than me at the far end of the quiet tasting room of Wolffer Estate Vineyards in Sagaponack, Long Island—his Argentinean tango shirt had caught my eye—it was clear that he was undertaking one of these extraordinary journeys. In sixty minutes over a flight of whites and reds, I learned that this Princeton grad had built a pharma start-up in the Bay Area, lectured at his alma mater about "Drug Dealers," competed in the Tango World Championship in Buenos Aires, mastered Brazilian jiu jitsu, attained fluency in five languages…the list continued. His boyish enthusiasm and curiosity reminded me of myself—yet his conviction and impressive capacity to follow through on all his ideas reminded me of how I *aspired* to be.

So what was he doing stateside after living all over the globe? Writing a book. He shared the proposed title with me as well as the concept—and I loved it. Moreover, it was clear that besides having reflected significantly on the content, he was already dedicating enormous time and effort to marketing strategies—where many talented writers and artists fall short. Throughout our conversation, he expounded on his ideas while politely responding to my queries, outlined his goals, and casually and confidently described the next steps he was taking to bring his project to fruition, the same unassuming way one might explain how to get to their local grocery. Six months later, I searched online and found that he had indeed published his book, just as planned. After another six months, I was not surprised to see that he'd topped *The New York Times* and *Wall Street Journal* bestseller lists. His book was *The Four Hour Workweek* (soon followed by *The Four Hour Body*). His name was Timothy Ferris.

Tim's success made me think of a similar encounter fifteen years earlier in Los Angeles. At a Halloween party hosted by a fellow Teach For America corps member, I ended up chatting most of the evening with a guy my age whose friend was doing TFA. This former Harvard student, clad in a white t-shirt and black beret for the festivities while I sported purple hair and orange shades, had moved to the west coast before graduating, not to teach, but to pursue acting. It's easy to roll your eyes when someone says that in LA, but he was different. He was bright, articulate, and grounded. As an undergrad, he'd already landed roles in the movies *School Ties* and *Geronimo* and now was sleeping on a buddy's couch while auditioning and writing a screenplay, trying to break through to the next level. Unlike the majority of Hollywood wannabes, he didn't name drop, possessed no airs, and spoke matter-of-factly about his next steps as a professional actor and aspiring writer. When the party ended, I wished him luck and we went our separate ways. Three years later while living in Rio de Janeiro, I went to the movies one night and immediately recognized him on the big screen. *Awesome.* He'd made it, just as planned. His film was *Goodwill Hunting*. His name? Matt Damon.

 BONUS ADVENTURES: www.MyTop40at40.com

- *Visit www.thefourhourworkweek.com*
- *See Kari with Matt Damon*
- *Hear Kari's commentary*

36

Crossing the Andes on Horseback

Six thrilling days, six thrilling hours

On the southern edge of Central Park in Manhattan, where Fifty-Ninth Street meets Sixth Avenue, lies a small plaza adorned with enormous bronze statues of the three "Great Liberators" of the Americas—José Martí in the Caribbean, Simón Bolívar in the northern part of South America, and José Francisco de San Martín in the southern part. One of the many unnoticed treasures tying New York City to the world, these statues remind me of one of my favorite trips, a holiday gift from my wife—an epic six-day, guided horseback crossing of the Andes in Argentina, a trip that traces the historic route General San Martín and his four thousand troops followed when they stormed Chile and defeated the surprised Spanish troops in 1817.

Our hodgepodge group on that trip consisted of Carlos, a sixty-year-old architect from Buenos Aires who had received a rare "free-pass" from his wife and kids to undertake this adventure; an extended family of nine from Cordoba, including an entomologist who, to the complete embarrassment of his family, spent part of every day crouched in his flaming red Speedo snapping close-ups of bees, beetles, and other mountain critters; the Mayor of the local province of Calingasta, in training for the upcoming *Extremo6000* adventure race in the Andes who had spent far more time on trails than behind a desk; our swashbuckling guide, Ramón, an Andean version of Crocodile Dundee with less polish but more brawn; Ramón's Sancho Panza—namely his son, Diego; one girlfriend each for guide and son; and five fearless muleteers who did most of the real work.

Our journey began ninety minutes outside of Barreal, a dusty town of no stoplights in Western Argentina that serves as the unofficial gateway to the Ruta San Martín. For the next six days, I was in outdoor heaven:

Six Thrilling Days

Day One: Just two hours into the trek, a mountain lion darted across our path thirty yards ahead. We broke into a gallop to pursue it, but in two quick jumps, this agile animal shot twenty feet up an embankment and disappeared behind the sandstone rocks. God spared nothing in designing that magnificent creature. Later that night, when we were all asleep under the stars, the horses—tied up liberally so they could roam to graze—shrieked frantically and broke into a thunderous stampede less than ten feet from my head.

A voice in the darkness, one of the muleteers, yelled, "*Qué paso?*" Then BANG! BANG! Our guide fired two shots from his rifle to scare away this same mountain lion, which had approached our camp in search of a late-night snack.

Day Two: We trotted and trudged our way over a fifteen-thousand-foot pass lined with "*penitentes*"—those stalagmite-like ice formations found in high altitudes. At the top, the mayor and I dismounted, left our horses to tag along with the pack, then hopped down the scree slope on the other side and continued running—and occasionally singing—several miles downhill into an enormous valley with sweeping views of the Andes and the twenty-three-thousand-foot Aconcagua in the distance. It was like *The Sound of Music* on steroids. That night our group slept on a sandy riverbank under the stars and rested both our feet and bottoms.

Day Three: Our first river crossings. On several occasions we forged the Mercedario River, which snakes through the Patos Sur Valley, with the water nearly reaching the saddle. Our horses hoisted their heads as high above the water as they could while we held on tight. One false step and our equine boat would float down river. In between these exhilarating crossings, we traversed flat, open terrain in an enormous valley that made even Big Sky Country seem small. We galloped at full-speed while jackrabbits and guanacos shot off in all directions. Untouchable Andean condors with their white-ringed necks and three-meter wingspans hovered serenely overhead, enjoying the best seats to this grand show. That night we feasted on grilled trout our muleteers had caught in one of the crystal-clear feeder streams.

Day Four: Our guide offered us a choice—ride up to the border of Chile where a non-descript sign indicated the demarcation, the official route of San Martín; or *say we did* and instead venture to the end of the valley to lunch at a small lake directly behind Aconcagua. We unanimously opted for the latter, the far more scenic option where we could even make out the trail heading to the summit of the Andean peak. I marveled that just four years earlier I'd struggled up that very trail never imagining that I'd return. Back at camp in gaucho fashion, we enjoyed yet another off-the-grid, off-the-clock evening of open-air *asado* (barbecue), *mate* (South American green tea drunk from a gourd that's passed around), and storytelling.

Day Five (Christmas): More galloping, more river crossings, and the beginning of our journey back. After dinner, to help celebrate the holiday, I pulled out my duty-free purchase of Jack Daniels, an instant hit and easily one of America's greatest ambassadors. Not an ounce was spared—and we all slumbered majestically.

Day Six: The long…long…march down…and out. We covered more than twenty miles and navigated thousands of feet of steep, hair-raising descents. Late morning I ran up one of the passes to give my fanny a reprieve, but ultimately there was no escaping the painful reality of travel by horseback—my legs and groin were shredded when we finally returned to our jeeps in the afternoon.

Six Thrilling Hours

Dark storm clouds approached during our final stretch to the jeeps, and by now it was raining hard in the mountains.

Our guide warned of flashfloods in the valley. Sure enough, as we headed toward town, we suddenly found ourselves driving through twelve inches of water. The dirt road had become a river basin and our jeep a kayak, navigating impromptu rapids as we bounced and chugged along with the current. After twenty minutes of Olympic water driving, we came to a rare sight—the *front* of the flashflood waters. The water and natural debris it transported advanced at twelve miles an hour while we jockeyed forward at fifteen, just fast enough to pull out in front and break away. We cruised the last ten miles safely on dry ground to our finish in Barreal and the beginning of a very long night.

I was scheduled to take the public mini-bus the following morning back to San Juan, but then I received an offer more appealing than the plodding, multiple-stop, six-hour cramped bus ride. Carlos, the architect, had arranged for a private taxi to drive him in the middle of the night to San Juan so he could catch his seven o'clock morning flight to Buenos Aires.

"Why don't you join me?" he suggested. It would be faster and more comfortable than the other options. I could stretch out in the back seat and it would be free—Carlos refused to take payment. I quickly accepted, asking one question: "Are you sure there will be space?"

"Of course!" he replied with customary Porteño confidence. "This is my *personal* taxi—I've rented the vehicle just for me." I had asked because a year earlier our own "private" taxi from the Mendoza airport to San Juan had contained a surprise passenger—a friend of the taxi driver.

"You don't mind, do you?" the driver had asked sheepishly. My wife and I simply went with the flow, squeezed in with everyone's luggage, and footed the bill for the group journey.

So I wasn't the least bit surprised when Carlos' private taxi arrived at 1:00 a.m., our designated departure time, with what appeared to be an additional body in the back seat. As we fumbled our way through the darkness toward the cab, we saw not one but three silhouettes. Already packed into the back seat were a rotund mother, her two-year-old son, and a pregnant woman curvier than any possible caricature who looked like she'd launch her baby any minute.

Carlos immediately protested, "*Pero qué es esto*? I thought this was my private taxi?"

The driver's innocent explanation: "*Es que*…this is my niece and she's supposed to see the doctor tomorrow morning for her final check-up (she was in her ninth month). I hope you don't mind if I give her (and her friend and friend's son) a ride."

There was no escape without seeming a heartless jerk. Carlos shut his mouth, we compressed the luggage as best we could, and we all got in. Carlos rode shotgun while I sardined myself into the back seat between the fat pregnant lady and the car door.

To make matters worse, our taxi was a rinky-dink Peugeot sedan that should have been retired fifteen years earlier, but was kept alive thanks to chewing gum, toothpicks, and other MacGyvering. Whether or not this rig could handle the excessive weight load remained to be seen.

My hopes were dashed when just ten minutes into the trip the motor sputtered to a stop. The flashflood waters had inundated the main highway through town, yet our taxi driver apparently hadn't thought twice about torpedo-ing us through the water. Midstream, he discovered he'd flooded the engine—literally. Our vehicle was stalled in the middle of the road—or river—at one thirty in the morning in complete darkness. Carlos was pulling his hair out and now feared missing his flight. I cracked my window desperate for a breath of fresh air and feared that my silent neighbor would suddenly scream out and produce an additional passenger.

The taxi driver waded through the water and lifted the hood. He didn't have a flashlight—why was I not sur-prised?—so I lent him my headlamp. Meanwhile, a bright red Coke delivery truck, our new beacon of hope, pulled up next to us as if in a too-good-to-be-true commercial. Carlos asked if we could hitch a ride to San Juan in the back of their truck. They weren't bound for San Juan, but they gladly helped tow us out of the water and lent us jumper cables to start the car. We'd lost ninety minutes, but we were back on track—Carlos could still catch his flight.

We zoomed down the highway, finally in a rhythm. The cumbia played, adrenaline dissipated, and conversation slowed. Carlos and I began to doze off. In fact, *everyone* be-gan to doze off, including our driver: our vehicle drifted left and swerved back right.

"*Voludo! Pero qué pasa?*" Carlos shouted at the driver, who confessed: "*Es que*...I didn't sleep a lot last night and...

well…I'm *pretty* tired…" Carlos and I sat bolt upright as if espresso were shot into our veins.

"Pull over!" Carlos commanded. We slowed to a stop in a gravel patch in the middle of nowhere.

"If I can just sleep for a little while I'll be fine," the driver assured us, hoping for a second chance. But only one solution remained: Carlos grabbed the wheel, I navigated shotgun, and in the back, fast asleep, snoring away for the next four hours were the friend, the toddler, the pregnant lady, and the cabbie.

Fortunately, everything worked out. Carlos just made his flight. The taxi driver caught some winks, assisted his niece, and still collected full-fare from Carlos. And me? I got another great story.

 BONUS ADVENTURES: www.MyTop40at40.com
- *See Crossing the Andes slideshow*
- *Hear Kari's commentary*

37

My Thirty-Six-Hour Inauguration Getaway
Watching history, sort of

In January of 2009, I had been a father all of two weeks, still adapting to the duties of my new role, when my wife—whose workload as a new mom far outweighed mine—gave the surprising green light to be part of a historic event: "You should go to DC this weekend."

She was referring to Obama's inauguration on the Mall. I hadn't even mentioned that earlier that week I'd scored tickets to one of the evening black tie Presidential Inaugural Balls. I didn't think twice about the thirty-six-hour furlough from home and work, and bolted.

Fueled by caffeine, conversation, and tunes, my cousin and I zipped three hundred twenty-five miles Monday night down to my buddy's pad in Arlington, Virginia, arriving after midnight. We arose early the next morning to discover glorious sunshine but a hope-busting temperature: twelve degrees, frigid enough to make *television* viewing of the Inauguration the popular choice among our crew, particularly since we'd be attending the Gala that evening. But I still had time for a run, and hell, the Mall was just five short miles away. I could go check out the scene and still return in time to watch the swearing-in ceremony. A ten-mile round trip run for history? Why not?

Geared up as best I could for the Arctic adventure, I trotted toward the Mall along the Custis Trail bike path, one of the many green corridors that lead surprisingly to the heart of the nation's capital. Mile by mile the path filled up with a family or church group here, a young couple or high school cross-country team there, with the buzz of fans off to The Big Game and the quiet, almost spiritual, resolution of pilgrims en route to Santiago de Compostela. I crossed the Potomac, snapped a quick photo for the family archives at the Lincoln Memorial, and then proceeded east toward the Capitol.

The electricity of the crowd and adrenaline got the best of me: *I have to stay here!* Leaving now seemed tantamount to entering the stadium for the World Cup final only to turn around and watch the game from home.

I dialed my cousin: "Change of plans."

I migrated with the masses as far as the Washington Monument, but could advance no further through the wall-to-wall people. For sixty minutes I hopped, huddled down from the howling wind, and even queued up unsuccessfully for coffee before aborting my mission and running back. Just how everyone else from all fifty states (Arizona? Florida?)

braved the Green Bay Packer temperatures, I have no clue. Perhaps the warmth of inspiration…

After watching the ceremony on TV, we taxied that evening to the Armory for the Southern Inaugural Ball, an especially fitting spot to celebrate the first African-American president, and spent the next few hours eating, drinking, and patriotically hobnobbing the way folks apparently do every four years in the elegantly adorned hall. While Derek Trucks jammed the blues, we jockeyed for position close to center stage.

At ten minutes to midnight, the real show began. Vice-President-elect Joe Biden, and his wife, Jill, walked on stage. A few remarks, one dance, and before we knew it, the dashing couple had disappeared. But now we were ready. Primed. Anxiously awaiting the grand entrance of Barack and Michelle Obama. On cue and provoking goosebumps, the 257th Army Band of the National Guard keyed up four Ruffles and Flourishes leading into "Hail to the Chief."

There he was: Barack Hussein Obama, the forty-fourth president of the United States of America. In the footsteps of George W., Clinton, Bush Senior, Reagan, and the rest of our nation's leaders, and the culmination of a remarkable journey. The flash of his proud smile matched the elegance of his white bow tie. Michelle Obama, equally elegant in her ruffled gown, stood by his side.

And that's when I observed the most fascinating part of the trip. Few guests looked directly at the president-elect and his wife during his brief speech or their twirl around the dance floor. Instead, nearly everyone stared at their smart phones or cameras, trying to record the event for posterity. During the six minutes that the Obamas graced the stage, the average guest actually *looked* at their new president for maybe a minute and spent the other five minutes viewing the spectacle through the medium of an electronic device.

Technology now allows us to be everywhere at all times connected to everyone else at the remarkable flip of a button. It's amazing. Yet the irony is that we are never fully *here* any more.*

We returned to my buddy's place at a quarter to three, and after downing a pot of strong coffee, my cousin and I hit the road north. After a quick seven o'clock shower at home, I commuted into the City for yet another day of work. It'd been a helluva thirty-six hours. I even had a few photos to prove it.☺

---

* An economist might aggregate enjoyment with an equation that looks something like this:

$aX + bY + cZ$ = E (Total Enjoyment Over Time), where X = Present Viewing Enjoyment (In the moment, with no other thoughts: "This is amazing!"), where Y = Present Shared Viewing Enjoyment (To buddy on cell phone: "Dude, you're *never* gonna guess where I am right now!"), where Z = Future (Stored) Viewing Enjoyment (To self or buddy in the future: "And this photo here was when the Obamas walked on stage!"), and a, b, and c are the coefficients of our attention which we control, where $a + b + c = 1$.

Today, folks are more like fifty percent in the moment (X) and split the rest of their attention between Y and Z ($.5X + .25Y + .25Z$). My overall enjoyment seems to peak if I'm about ninety percent in the moment and ten percent focused on storage ($.9X + .0Y + .1Z$). I soak up the experience as best as I can, taking in the chills and thrills first-hand, and shoot just a few quick photos to remember the experience and share it later with friends.

 Bonus Adventures: www.MyTop40at40.com

- *See Inauguration Getaway slideshow*
- *Hear Kari's commentary*

38

Arrested!

Unfortunate coincidences lead to cuffs and a courtroom

O ne thousand one…one thousand two…one thousand three…one thousand four…one thousand five, and just like that, New York State Trooper Ramsey had frisked me, confiscated my wallet and phone, and—CLINK! CHINK! CLICK! CLICK!—handcuffed me to a non-descript iron bar on the police station wall. You had to admire his efficiency, as well as the sheen of my silver shackles, evidently in use for the first time. I wasn't quite sure how I'd gotten into this legal predicament, but eventually I'd sort it out.

It all started earlier that cold March morning in 2009 when my cousin, Mark, joined me for an innocent Sunday hike up Bear Mountain, forty-five minutes north of New York

City. Because this was his first physical activity in a long while, we ascended gently, pausing frequently along the relatively steep trail to allow him to catch his breath. But when we finally reached the summit—which sounds more grandiose than it is since you can also drive to the top—we immediately faced three challenges: First, my cousin's Achilles was shot—he had limped the final quarter-mile to the top; Second, it had taken us two hours to summit when it should have taken us only forty minutes and I feared it would now take us even longer to descend with his gimpy leg; And third, snow was forecasted— if a whiteout caught us halfway down the mountain, we'd be in real trouble. We had to change our plan. Quickly.

I gave my cousin my hat, fleece jacket, and thermos of hot Gatorade and settled him comfortably on a bench, then took off down the trail, intending to return in thirty minutes with the car up the access road. But as I sprinted down the mountain, it suddenly dawned on me: *The access road might be locked*. With my adrenaline pumping and mind racing, I reached the car in just ten minutes.

As luck would have it, a state police car idled in the parking lot nearby, so I asked the officer about the summit access road. As I had feared, it was closed. I calmly explained that if I didn't get my cousin off the mountain using the road, we very well might need to be airlifted off later should inclement weather strike. At that point, he called in the sheriff, who arrived in her patrol car a minute later. Although she wouldn't allow *me* to use the access road, she agreed to send another officer to get Mark. I promptly called Mark on his cell to share the good news.

Relieved that everything now seemed under control, I stretched on the ground while the first officer filed an incident report. He took my driver's license and asked me some basic questions about Mark and myself. But a few minutes later the officer called the sheriff over to his car. Long pause, then he said, "Sir, it says here your license is suspended in the state of New York. Do you know anything about this?"

I had no clue what he was talking about. In fact, since I am frequently mistaken for Latino by my last name (look up "Loya" in a phone directory and you'll usually discover Alberto Loya, Carlos Loya, etc.) and for a woman by my first name (I've actually *won* races in the female categories before race officials realized their mistake), my first thought was that I'd been confused with someone else. The officer then referenced two outstanding tickets in Brooklyn from three years earlier and asked if I knew anything about these. I didn't. I couldn't remember any traffic violations other than two parking tickets in Manhattan.

At this point, the sheriff took over the interrogation: "So I don't get this…" she proceeded suspiciously, "You have a *California* driver's license listing a *New York* address, and now you're telling me you live in *New Jersey*?"

It was true—and indeed unique. I had renewed my license in California during the summer between my first and second year of business school and they had printed my New York address, and I'd recently moved to New Jersey. She then fired off question after question as if trying to ensnare a serial conman in his lies:

"How long have you lived there?"

"What do you do for a living?"

"Do you have any proof of your address in New Jersey?"

And then a strange one: "How much money do you have in your wallet?"

I generally used plastic for any expense over five dollars and rarely carried cash, but I happened to hit the ATM that morning.

"Forty bucks," I replied.

"That's all?" she responded in disbelief, as if my wallet might contain a wad of unmarked bills to incriminate me.

She asked me to retrieve the paperwork from my vehicle. I walked around to the passenger side and, for the first time, felt uncomfortable. With the first officer carefully positioned a yard behind me to my left and the sheriff four yards to my right, the officer began spoon-feeding me instructions: "Please open the vehicle door. Please open the glove compartment. Now please take out the insurance document. Now please hand that to me."

I fancied that the insurance papers which listed our New Jersey address might exonerate me and end this unexpected drama, but the sheriff quickly quashed my hope: "Please surrender your keys to Officer Ramsey." Anything with *surrender* never bodes well.

Minutes later, I was cuffed to the wall in the state police precinct, conveniently located at the far end of the Bear Mountain parking lot. Judging by the facial expressions of the other young officers on duty, I was one of the few "criminals" of the day, if not the entire winter season, and a welcome escape from their office drudgery. Moreover, my appearance didn't exactly scream criminal—winter running gear; no tattoos, scars, piercings, or cigarettes; and a genuine smile that said "Hi, how are you?" and not "GIT the FUCK AWAY from me o' I gonna BUST YO' ASS!"

Had this happened ten years earlier, I might have panicked. *What will my parents say? Will I ever get a job again? Am I going to prison?* Instead, I had a clean conscience and treated this more like yet another interesting adventure, curious how it would all unfold.

When Mark and the other officer eventually returned to the station, oblivious to everything that had transpired, they strutted through the station door toward me prompting the sheriff to lay down the law: "Sir, you need to return to the lobby! You cannot be here with *the prisoner.*"

I, the aforementioned prisoner, quickly blurted out, "Mark, everything is fine. We'll sort this out!"

Twenty minutes later, I'd posted one hundred dollars bail, signed the proper forms agreeing to my court date, and retrieved my possessions. Since my license remained suspended, Mark drove me home. My first call after regaining my freedom was to my wife who was in Houston at the time.

"Sweetie?"

"Sí, amor."

"Do you by any chance remember any traffic tickets? Like from a few years ago in Brooklyn?"

She reminded me that we had received a couple tickets just before entering the Battery Park Tunnel from Brooklyn for not installing our front license plate or displaying our New York State registration sticker, even though both were in the glove compartment. But she assured me that she had paid them immediately—she handled all of our car-related matters.

"*Por qué? Dónde estás?*"

"Well, I'm fine now…but…a little while ago I was…sort of…arrested."

"*Qué?!!! Pero cómo?!!!*" You have to be very careful about what you say to a Latin woman. The only thing faster and more efficient than the Internet is a Latin American female gossip chain.

Early the next morning I called the New York DMV and discovered that I indeed had two unpaid tickets from May of 2006. The tickets had been for failure to have the front license plate mounted (one hundred dollars) and failure to post the New York State inspection (ninety dollars), just as my wife had suspected. But I also discovered that several days later the DMV had received a check from my wife for one hundred dollars instead of one hundred ninety dollars—she had written the check for the wrong amount. The DMV had applied fifty dollars toward each ticket, and then suspended my license after one month when they hadn't received full payment. Since my address changes had outpaced the DMV's records, I never received any notifications. I promptly paid the outstanding balance on both tickets online.

Now I had to prepare myself for the April 16 court date. My particular citation was 511-1A, a misdemeanor, for "Aggravated Unlicensed Operation of a motor vehicle in the Third Degree," for which there were three possible outcomes:

1) a fine between two hundred dollars and five hundred dollars; 2) a jail sentence up to thirty days; or 3) a combination of (1) and (2). "Jail" didn't sound good.

The Stony Point Courthouse sat on a little green hill in the middle of a Lake Wobegone town with proud ties to the American Revolution and where everyone likely knew the judge, the minister, and the town drunk. The day we arrived the courtroom held a healthy mix of twenty-five locals—largely officials on duty who bantered away with each other as if at a weekend social—and twenty-five out-of-towners who anxiously sat in silence awaiting their fate. Besides me, only five men wore suits: the judge underneath his black robe, the district attorney, a private lawyer, the public defender, and one baby-faced seventeen-year-old with a messy list of charges that no fancy Armani suit could ever wipe clean.

After two hours of cases involving *repeated drunk driving, assault, reckless driving, resisting arrest* and other charges that made me feel like a saint, I finally heard my name: "Loya."

I rose, stepped forward, and the judge swore me in. Like with the previous cases, the DA mechanically recited the charges from his dossier, then turned to a second sheet and added, "It appears that the defendant already paid the balance on the original tickets, so we recommend commuting the sentence to a fine."

At this point, the judge nodded at me and asked, "Mr. Loya, how do you plead?"

I looked squarely at the judge and delivered my rehearsed line, "Not guilty, Your Honor." For the first time in two hours, the DA lifted his head from his stack of papers and examined me as if I had burst out singing. He gazed back at the judge, seeking guidance. The judge paused, then with equal parts gravitas and equanimity said, "Mr. Loya, *do you understand* what is being offered?"

I held my ground: "Yes, Your Honor, and I am not guilty."

He clearly was not expecting this response: "You do understand that this means going to trial, and that means taking the testimony of the officers involved…" This deviation from the precise playbook clearly had flustered the DA, who now listened attentively.

I elaborated: "Well, as I understand it, the key question is whether or not I was *aware or had reason to be aware* of my expired driver's license…" With growing exasperation, the judge cut me off: "Gentlemen, please approach the bench!"

I stepped to the front of the courtroom and made my case: First, I had approached the officers soliciting their help—they had not stopped me for any violation. Would I really have approached them if I had known my license had been suspended? Second, the original violation three years earlier had been paid, just not paid in full. Simply an innocent mistake. As soon as I found out about it, I paid it the next day.

"Man!" the judge interrupted me, breaking character with a shout, "You call *that* a whisper?" I wasn't quite sure what to say.

"Geez…" he continued, "*Your* voice carries more than *mine!*"

I took that as my cue to chime in, "Well, I *do* do voice-overs professionally." Instantly I felt the mood lighten. The judge and I were suddenly buddies in casual conversation.

"Hmmm.. interesting...You do that in LA?"

"LA, here in New York, and other places as well..."

As we chatted, the DA pulled another file—the officer's arrest report—then huddled over it with the judge, mumbling.

"Now you say you were hiking?" inquired the judge, turning back to me.

"Yes, Your Honor. But my cousin had a problem with his foot, so I went to get help."

More mumbling between the DA and the judge, then, "Shall we forget this?" Pause.

"Yeah." Pause.

The judge looked at both of us, "Okay, gentlemen, please return to your places."

I returned to my original spot behind the defendant's table. The judge, now back in formal character, said, "Mr. District Attorney, do we have a motion to dismiss the charge?"

The DA promptly responded, "Yes, sir," to which the judge concluded, "Okay. Charges dismissed!" and banged his gavel.

He finally proclaimed, "Mr. Loya, you may approach the court clerk and arrange for your bail money to be returned." It was as simple as that, and a week later I received a check for one hundred dollars from the County Clerk.

The whole incident was a good test of a marriage. After all, if you're wife gets you arrested and you still love her, it's gotta be a decent match. The incident also made me revisit my answer to a fundamental question: "What is most important in life?" For years I have responded in order—Health, Family, Friends. But since March 1, 2009, I have answered with a resounding new number one: Liberty!

BONUS ADVENTURES: www.MyTop40at40.com
- *See Kari's Pre-Arraignment Bail Record*
- *Hear Kari's commentary*

39

Patagonia and Fatherhood

Hiking in southern Chile resembles the first year as a dad

I don't care what anyone tells you—the first year of fatherhood can be brutal. You step on a fast-paced treadmill of diapers, feedings, crying, more crying, and an unpredictable smattering of spit-ups and other disasters. Throw in the logistics of frequent doctor visits, unexpected health issues, and daycare—and you wonder why any sane individual, including your parents, would ever put up with all of this.

You also understand immediately why so many friends with kids suddenly disappear. All attention—other than cerebral RAM reserved for work—becomes focused on the baby. And this usually comes at the expense of much-needed time with spouse, time with friends, and time for self. The short shift in priorities makes sense—I totally get that. But I was amazed at how many people with kids under four years old had never spent more than twenty-four hours away from their children, either with just their wife, their friends, or even by themselves. The right combination of extra hands, time, and money seemed too elusive.

So when year one of parenthood concluded, and I had the rare chance to spend a week solo hiking and kayaking in Patagonia while my wife and daughter visited family in Argentina, I took it. My starting point was Punta Arenas, the sleepy constellation of inns, squares, and lighthouses on the Straits of Magellan where you feel like you're at the edge of the world. The outbound flights listed on the departure board at the airport confirmed the feeling: *Antarctica. Antarctica.* Puerto Montt. *Antarctica.* El Cafayate. *Antarctica.*

Pit, pat, pit, pat, pit, pat. The hail ricocheted off me and my bivy. I was smack in the middle of a Southern hemisphere Patagonian summer—Mark Twain clearly never spent a summer *here*—and just forty-eight hours into my journey, I'd already swallowed a hard dose of character-building Patagonian reality. First, my rental car's battery had died in Puerto Natales where I had to conscript two bus drivers to help push and jump start the VW. Then on the gravel road in the Torres Del Paine National Park, I'd shredded a tire so I had to replace it with the emergency limited-range spare. And now I'd trekked the first stretch of the fabled W route only to collapse exhausted, hungry, and shivering into my bivy. *Was this really how I'd chosen to spend Christmas?*

The next morning was no better. I arose at four in the morning to ascend for an hour to the *mirador* and watch the golden sunrise on the iconic granite towers—those captured in

213

the Patagonia apparel company's logo. Only the hail had turned to snow. And more snow. And more snow. For two hours I sat amidst grey clouds and fought off shivers with my one luxury: three packs of Starbucks' recently-introduced Via instant coffee.

The storied towers shot up a hundred meters from me across a frigid lake—I just couldn't see them. Like a sex-starved teen on a tropical beach, I stared and stared, waiting for Mother Nature to reveal herself—first the base of her breasts, then a bit of cleavage between the north and central tower, and…just a little more…just a wee bit more…But no! No nipple. The clouds never cleared and I left, denied.

But late that afternoon everything suddenly came into perspective and I realized that hiking in Patagonia was the perfect metaphor for fatherhood. You slog through an incessant, icy wind; hail smacks you in the face; a brief downpour forces you to double-up your rain gear; then another austral gust of wind buffets you from both sides. And just when you are about to throw in the towel and abandon the hike, the wind dies, the sky clears, and the sun illuminates what is easily one of the most spectacular places on the planet: Lakes glisten with colors so green and blue that a Disney animator would be hard-pressed to replicate the scene; Intricately-shaped granite massifs tower above as if God took the spectacular Canadian Rockies and decided to sculpt a few centerpieces; Glaciers and their cities of ice sprawl up mountainsides and cascade into the waters below; Andean condors soar high above like angels keeping watch over their treasured playground.

"This is the most amazing thing ever," you say to yourself in complete awe.

And the first time your baby girl smiles at you and rests her head gently on your chest, you utter those same words: *This is the most amazing thing ever.* Nothing else matters. Nothing at all. You are a daddy. And it's the best damn thing in the whole wide world!

 Bonus Adventures: www.MyTop40at40.com

- *See Patagonia slideshow*
- *Watch baby announcement trailer*
- *Hear Kari's commentary*

40

Four Great Ways to See the Big Apple

Running, climbing, kayaking, and skiing Manhattan

M anhattan is an island of concrete, steel, brick, and glass and most residents and visitors navigate its streets in one of four ways: by walking, subway, taxi, or for the deep-pocketed and thrill-seekers, even helicopter. But if your preferred mode of travel involves pumping the heart and burning the lungs, an entirely different Big Apple *Grand Slam* awaits you—four super cool *athletic* ways to see The City.

Run the New York City Marathon
The marathon is undoubtedly *the* signature New York City athletic event and the world's best-known marathon. Think of it like your own healthy, sightseeing tour of the City

where forty thousand amped souls from all over the world join in and a couple million spectators cheer you on. Not a bad way to spend the day. I was lucky enough to enjoy one of those days in November of 2002 when I managed to secure a coveted race number through the lottery.

I didn't exactly train for the marathon. Cursed with flat feet, I'm limited by how much time I can run, particularly on pavement. My training consisted of a bit of soccer, a number of short jogs, and a couple "make-sure-I-can-finish" two-hour runs to prevent disaster. My real goal was to get on and off the course quickly and have a good time in the process, so I donned the same low-tech garb I used to run Pamplona—thin white cotton pants, a bright red sash belt, a white cotton shirt, and my San Fermín handkerchief draped around my neck. My final touch was a rolled up copy of the Sunday *New York Times* so I could occasionally look backwards and, in Pamplona tradition, "taunt the bulls." Nothing like a good costume to make some friends—a group of Spaniards at the start caught sight of my outfit and immediately burst into Pamplona song. *Uno de enero! Dos de febrero! Tres de marzo! Cuatro de abril! Cinco de mayo! Seis de junio! Siete de Julio! San Fermín!!* And then we were off…

The run itself is a blur of memories: first storming the Verrazano Bridge with forty thousand warriors; then dancing across it to Sinatra's "New York, New York" as we gazed at the Statue of Liberty and lower Manhattan skyline; cruising down Fourth Avenue in Brooklyn where crowds piled up brownstone steps, onto friends' shoulders, and even onto rooftops to show their support; crossing the Queensboro

217

bridge into Manhattan feeling like a superhero and floating through the roar of the crowd on First Avenue.

Then comes the painful realization that seven miles of slogging remain as you leave Manhattan for the Bronx where crowds nearly vanish and mental toughness becomes a major factor. Next, feeling the buzz of Central Park, the teaser rolling hills that keep you honest, the celebratory jaunt along Central Park South, and the unexpectedly uphill stretch from Columbus Circle toward the finish that exacts one last push from every competitor. And finally…crossing the finish line, where one of the incredibly well-organized volunteers wraps you in a heat blanket and drapes a well-deserved medal around your neck. Your feet may burn, your knees may throb, and your muscles may scream "Uncle!"—but nothing medicates better than the thrill of victory.

Climb to the Top of the Empire State Building

If running around the City doesn't excite you, try running to the top of it. The Empire State Building Run-Up, in which I competed in early 2002, is an entirely different beast. For starters, instead of taking place on a leisurely Saturday or Sunday, it took place on a Tuesday morning, exacting a sacrifice from nearly every participant (I cut class at business school to attend). Furthermore, instead of being held in the warmer spring or fall, it occurred in the dead of February, the bleakest month for New York City tourism when ice, bitter cold, and long faces prevail. Runners arrived all bundled in scarves, hats, gloves and coats.

After passing through metal detectors, we shed our winter layers, then piled on top of each other in the lobby like roaches, waiting for the start. This was the twenty-fifth anniversary of the event, so even more television reporters and spectators than usual crammed into the gaps. My fellow competitors largely sported what looked like a mix-and-match collection from the past four decades—recycled and crumpled outfits that seemed as much about sentimentality as functionality. If grit had a fashion line, this would have been it.

Runners were divided into just four groups—slow women, slow men, fast women, fast men. And rather than staggered starts, a mass start released each group, with only a minute between each start. The race organizers must have calculated the rental cost of occupying part of the building on a weekday and quickly realized they needed to compress the event as much as possible—after all, time is money!

But from a runner's standpoint, the race became a painful, if not comedic, free-for-all. Imagine squeezing in with fifty runners onto a starting line thirty feet wide, then sprinting twenty yards toward the stairwell opening just five feet wide, knowing that only two from your pack will make it through unscathed while the rest splatter against the wall and doorframe like a strange Pollack painting. Once we managed to untangle our limbs and enter the stairwell, the first five flights were more bumper cars than race. Passing was next-to-impossible given the concentration of runners and frequent turns of the staircase.

Then there was the burn. Not just the leg burn—that was to be expected. But after thirty flights, the lung burn—and not the clean, *I've-run-real-fast* lung burn, but the *I'm-*

sucking-down-asbestos-in-this-seventy-year-old-stairwell lung burn. It was awful, like slurping sawdust instead of Gu all the way to the top.

For the survivors, nonetheless, glory was granted on the eighty-sixth floor observation deck. I bolted out of the stairwell into the crisp morning air of a beautiful twenty-degree sunny day and ran from one corner of the deck nearly all the way around clockwise with the City at my feet: the Statue of Liberty to the west, Central Park to the north, the Chrysler Building to the east, and finally the finish line as I turned south. It was a spectacular victory lap followed by refreshments one floor down. It was also a fitting reminder that "If you can make it here, you can make it anywhere."

Kayak around the Statue of Liberty

A third great way to see the City is not by land, but by sea—or river and sound to be precise. After just one pre-requisite class, you can paddle with a group by kayak down the Hudson, around the Statue of Liberty, and back up the West Side. So on a gorgeous, seventy-five degree Sunday afternoon in August, I joined a guide and eight others as we plopped into the river near Twenty-Fifth Street in search of unique City views without the stress of crowds, taxis, or noise.

We coasted a mile south hugging the Manhattan side of the river while admiring the dreamy Frank Gehry-designed, glass IAC building and other recent additions to the skyline. Then we completed a group crossing to the Jersey side of the river, dodging tugboats, river cruises, sailboats, and other vessels plying this busy waterway. Finally, we paddled for the far side of Liberty Island braving swells, currents, and the wakes of Liberty and Ellis Island cruise ships shuttling tourists to and from the historic landmarks.

The trip was amazingly peaceful. Seagulls sang overhead. The semi-brackish air slapped us playfully while muffling most sounds beyond our paddling party. The warm sunshine reflected off the water and ensured we'd all come away with a golden tan. Through the four-hour adventure, we enjoyed amazing shots of Lady Liberty, spectacular views of Lower Manhattan, and a fantastic upper body workout—a delightful afternoon.

Cross-Country Ski through Times Square

To complete the Big Apple *Grand Slam* requires luck—and a big wave surfer's readiness to seize the moment. Since New York City is not tucked neatly inland like Buffalo or Syracuse, it doesn't get tons of snow (excepting the last two years!). In fact, Hollywood films showing those white Christmases in New York represent the exception, not the rule. On several late nights in midwinter, I've even stumbled across large-scale sets of white sheets, synthetic "fluffiness," and truckloads of imported snow in Central Park where a film crew was busy capturing that "magical" white Christmas moment.

Making this *Grand Slam* even more difficult is the competition—the hundreds if not thousands of city snowplowers, high-rise doormen, and sledding six-year-olds who are just as eager to catch that rare wave and do their own thing. In impressive fashion, the first two groups sweep, blow, and scrape nearly every sidewalk and street, making life easier for the pedestrian but rendering your winter snow wave impossible to ride. The poor souls whose cars are parked on the street become the ultimate losers, *caught inside*, struggling to remove the snow from their vehicles and escape before another wave—a twelve-inch coat of gritty ice and packed snow from the street plows—buries them for days.

So on Saturday night, February 11, 2006 when I was living on Ninetieth and Broadway and the snow started to dump, I knew I'd have a very small window early the next morning to catch my wave. Sure enough, nearly a foot had fallen by morning light and the *Blizzard of '06* would continue to cripple the City through the early afternoon, leaving twenty-seven inches of snow in Central Park amidst howling winds, terrible visibility, and snow drifts that threatened to engulf anything outside. In other words, it was perfect.

Like a six-year-old on Christmas morning, I sprang out of bed. Within minutes, I donned my cross-country skis— *Please Lord give me a good reason why I'm storing these in my tiny New York City apartment*—and by seven in the morning I was cruising through Central Park. To my delight, few souls had ventured out into the white fury and the streets, paths, and sidewalks remained covered with snow. Even when I reached the southern edge of the Park at Fifty-Ninth Street, snow blanketed everything.

And that's when I did what few folks will ever have the opportunity to do—ski down the middle of Seventh Avenue right through Times Square, the heart of New York City and arguably the capital of the world. Below me just white, white,

white and the *whoosh, whoosh, whoosh* of my skis. Above me, a kaleidoscope of color and lights on a surreal canvas of ivory and ash, as if Gaugin, Monet, and Van Gogh had collaborated to paint the blizzard sky. And next to me? A couple of lone ducks—bright-yellow taxis fishtailing forward, the turbaned drivers as amazed at their strange new road companion as at the blizzard itself.

I was in a magical zone. Even though I sported classic skis, I surged with adrenaline and began skate skiing—it just felt cooler. I rode *the monster wave* down Seventh Avenue as camera-toting tourists snapped away, continued all the way to Fourteenth Street, cut east to Union Square, then shot back uptown on the boutique-lined Madison Avenue. By the time I arrived on the Upper East Side near Eighty-Sixth Street ready to cross the Park, my wave had fizzled—the competition was now out in full-force parceling up the ski course. But no matter. While I'll never hold a candle to Laird Hamilton and his feats off the North Shore or at Teahupo'o in Tahiti, I had caught my own epic, once-in-a-lifetime *New York City wave*—and completed my Big Apple Athletic *Grand Slam*.

 BONUS ADVENTURES: www.MyTop40at40.com

- *See Empire State Building Run Up race number*
- *See Kari at marathon finish*
- *Hear Kari's commentary*

EPILOGUE

So that's it, the halfway point—at least according to the life expectancy of the average American. I now face a receding hairline, creaky knees, and the daily struggle to balance work-family-friends-play, but these are mere details. At forty, I'm more excited than ever to make the second half as good if not better than the first.

Part of that enthusiasm comes from living with what I call a *story paradigm*. When you think about telling a story of what you are going through, you develop a writer's acuity for detail in the moment: the smell of an old trunk, the thud of a soccer ball, the shimmer of a new toy, the soft ripples of corduroy, the aftertaste of lemon, the memory of a teenage concert, or the odd titillation of danger. Everything becomes more intense.

Second, a story paradigm can pull you through tough times—imagining yourself in the future sharing your experience can help uncover the humor, lesson, or silver lining in almost any circumstances.

The question that came up most, though, during the writing and editing of this book was, "What have I learned?" It's simple: I understand more clearly what makes me happy. The latest version of my *Mission Statement* in the Appendix

224

guides my decisions and actions and helps make my days more meaningful and more fun. I hope the forty stories in this collection reflect these principles at work.

The other question that arose, of course, was, "What's next?" I have an ever-expanding list of cool ideas which I hope to make reality—biking across the country with my dad, making a short film with my daughter, traveling through the Middle East with my wife, creating a children's book with my mom and sister, samba dancing through the 2014 World Cup in Brazil with friends...Ultimately, however, it's not about *doing*, it's about *being*, and that means a focus on living my Mission, whether I'm in the Amazon jungle or a hospital bed, so that my best years lie ahead. See you at fifty!

APPENDIX

My Mission Statement (as of December 2011)

Hoo ha!—Radiate positive energy
- Focus on possibilities, not problems
- Focus on what I'm doing, not what I'm *not* doing
- Focus on strengths, not weaknesses
- Focus on similarities, not differences

Be Real—Tell it like it is

Be Responsible—Do what needs to be done

Be Adventurous—Take risks, love challenges,
and try new things

Listen—Try to understand (others and myself)

Be Patient—Bird by bird (a la Anne Lamott)

Be Present—*Aqui e agora* (*Here and now,* like the Brazilians)

Be Helpful

ACKNOWLEDGMENTS

This story project was especially fun and meaningful because I connected with and learned from an extraordinary cast of characters behind the scenes. I owe enormous thanks to the individuals below who provided invaluable feedback on everything from story content and book design to overall business concept and strategies. It's amazing what can be accomplished when great people are involved. *Citius! Altius! Fortius!*

Shaila Abdullah ★ John Addrizzo ★ Rodrigo Allub ★ Sue Bastian ★ Dave Belden ★ Rachael Bennett ★ Peter Briggs ★ Mark Bruno ★ Tony Byrd ★ Sydney Colburn ★ Matt Compton ★ Jon Connorton ★ Ben Cox ★ Ira Gottlieb ★ Stephanie Gunning ★ Michele Hoos ★ Sarui Jaled ★ Mark Kerback ★ Alex Kitzis ★ Jay Klein ★ Matt Komonchak ★ Erin Kornfeld ★ Claire Lea Howarth ★ Erica Leone ★ Kristin Loya ★ Merv Loya ★ Nancy Loya ★ David Lyerly ★ Chris MacPherson ★ Pete McBride ★ Audrey Miller ★ Jim Miller ★ Christian Molstrom ★ Sandy Osborne ★ Azra Osmanovic ★ Vedad Osmanovic ★ Judy Parris ★ Kristin Pate ★ Betty Perrin ★ Andres Pintor ★ Mark Reardon ★ Jon Rettmann ★ Henry Robles ★ Ralph Saltus ★ Paul Sanders ★ Kari Schwartz ★ Stephen Spahn ★ Ellen Stein ★ Susy Struble ★ Rich Wazacz ★ John Weinkopf ★ Wallace Zane

CPSIA information can be obtained at www.ICGtesting.com
Printed in the USA
BVOW071648150412

287654BV00002B/2/P